Third Workshop on Multilingual Surface Realisation (MSR 2020)

Held online due to COVID-19

Barcelona, Spain
12 December 2020

ISBN: 978-1-7138-2832-7

Printed from e-media with permission by:

Curran Associates, Inc.
57 Morehouse Lane
Red Hook, NY 12571

Some format issues inherent in the e-media version may also appear in this print version.

Printed with permission by Curran Associates, Inc. (2021)

For permission requests, please contact the Association for Computational Linguistics at the address below.

Association for Computational Linguistics
209 N. Eighth Street
Stroudsburg, Pennsylvania 18360

Phone: 1-570-476-8006
Fax: 1-570-476-0860

acl@aclweb.org

Additional copies of this publication are available from:

Curran Associates, Inc.
57 Morehouse Lane
Red Hook, NY 12571 USA
Phone: 845-758-0400
Fax: 845-758-2633
Email: curran@proceedings.com
Web: www.proceedings.com

COLING 2020

Multilingual Surface Realisation

Proceedings of the Third Workshop

December 12, 2020
Barcelona, Spain (Online)

Organisers

Simon Mille, Pompeu Fabra University
Anya Belz, University of Brighton
Bernd Bohnet, Google Inc.
Thiago Castro Ferreira, Federal University of Minas Gerais
Yvette Graham, ADAPT, Trinity College Dublin
Leo Wanner, ICREA/Pompeu Fabra University

Program Committee:

Miguel Ballesteros, IBM Research, USA
Valerio Basile, Torino University, Italy
Alberto Bugarín, University of Santiago de Compostela, Spain
Wenchao Du, Carnegie Mellon University, USA
William Dyer, Oracle Corporation, USA
Henry Elder, ADAPT Center DCU, Ireland
Farhood Farahnak, Concordia University, Canada
Kim Gerdes, Sorbonne Nouvelle, France
Xudong Hong, MPI Informatics and Saarland University, Germany
Yannis Konstas, Heriot Watt University, UK
Emiel Krahmer, Tilburg University, The Netherlands
Guy Lapalme, RALI, Universit de Montral, Canada
Elena Lloret, Universitat d'Alacant, Spain
Alessandro Mazzei, Torino University, Italy
Ryan McDonald, Google Research, USA
David McDonald, Sift Inc., USA
Joakim Nivre, Uppsala University, Sweden
Laura Perez, Pompeu Fabra University, Spain
Yevgeniy Puzikov, TU Darmstadt, Germany
Gabor Recksi, TU Wien, Austria
Leonardo Ribeiro, TU Darmstadt, Germany
Horacio Saggion, Pompeu Fabra University, Spain
Anastasia Shimorina, LORIA, France
Aleksander Shvets, Pompeu Fabra University, Spain
Xiang Yu, University of Stuttgart, Germany
Yue Zhang, Westlake University, China

Invited Speaker:

Yue Zhang, Westlake University

Table of Contents

Conference Program

December 12, 2020

14.00–14.15 Opening

14.15–15.00 Invited talk: Yue Zhang

15.00–15.30 SR'20 Overview and evaluation results

The Third Multilingual Surface Realisation Shared Task (SR'20): Overview and Evaluation Results
Simon Mille, Anya Belz, Bernd Bohnet, Thiago Castro Ferreira, Yvette Graham and Leo Wanner

15.50–17.00 Q&A with authors

BME-TUW at SR'20: Lexical grammar induction for surface realization
Gábor Recski, Ádám Kovács, Kinga Gémes, Judit Ács and Andras Kornai

ADAPT at SR'20: How Preprocessing and Data Augmentation Help to Improve Surface Realization
Henry Elder

IMSurReal Too: IMS in the Surface Realization Shared Task 2020
Xiang Yu, Simon Tannert, Ngoc Thang Vu and Jonas Kuhn

Lexical Induction of Morphological and Orthographic Forms for Low-Resourced Languages
Taha Tobaili

NILC at SR'20: Exploring Pre-Trained Models in Surface Realisation
Marco Antonio Sobrevilla Cabezudo and Thiago Pardo

Surface Realization Using Pretrained Language Models
Farhood Farahnak, Laya Rafiee, Leila Kosseim and Thomas Fevens

December 12, 2020 (continued)

17:00–18:00 Round table

18.00–18.15 Closing

The Third Multilingual Surface Realisation Shared Task (SR'20): Overview and Evaluation Results

Simon Mille
UPF, Barcelona
simon.mille@upf.edu

Anya Belz
University of Brighton
a.s.belz@brighton.ac.uk

Bernd Bohnet
Google Inc.
bohnetbd@google.com

Thiago Castro Ferreira
Fed. Univ. Minas Gerais
thiago.castro.ferreira@gmail.com

Yvette Graham
ADAPT, Trinity College Dublin
ygraham@tcd.ie

Leo Wanner
ICREA/UPF, Barcelona
leo.wanner@upf.edu

Abstract

This paper presents the results of the Third Shared Task on Multilingual Surface Realisation (SR'20) which was organised as part of the COLING'20 Workshop on Multilingual Surface Realisation. As in SR'18 and SR'19, the shared task comprised two tracks: (1) a Shallow Track where the inputs were full UD structures with word order information removed and tokens lemmatised; and (2) a Deep Track where additionally, functional words and morphological information were removed. Moreover, each track had two subtracks: (a) restricted-resource, where only the data provided or approved as part of a track could be used for training models, and (b) open-resource, where any data could be used. The Shallow Track was offered in 11 languages, whereas the Deep Track in 3. Systems were evaluated using automatic metrics and direct assessment by human evaluators of Readability and Meaning Similarity to reference outputs. We present the evaluation results, along with descriptions of the SR'20 tracks, data and evaluation methods, as well as brief summaries of the participating systems. Full descriptions of the participating systems can be found in separate system reports elsewhere in this volume.

1 Introduction

SR'20 is the fourth in a line of shared tasks focused on surface realisation, the name originally given to the last stage in the first-generation (pre-statistical and pre-neural) Natural Language Generation (NLG) pipeline, mapping from semantic representations to fully realised surface word strings. When we ran the first Surface Realisation Shared Task in 2011 (Belz et al., 2011), it was to address a situation where there were many different approaches to SR but none of them were comparable. We developed a common-ground input representation that different approaches could map their normal inputs to, making results directly comparable for the first time. Most SR'11 systems (and all top performing ones) were statistical dependency realisers that did not make use of an explicit, pre-existing grammar. However, the question of how inputs to the realisers were going to be provided in an embedding system was left open.

By the time we proposed the second SR Task (Mille et al., 2017), Universal Dependencies (UDs) had emerged as a convenient standard in parsing, with many associated data sets, that we were able to pick up and use as the common-ground representation. By now, the third, neural generation of NLG methods was beginning to dominate the field, and systems participating in SR'18 were all trained to map directly from the UD inputs to the surface strings by some form of neural method. The question of how inputs to the realisers were going to be supplied remained open; moreover, most current approaches to NLG no longer even distinguished a separate surface realisation stage. Nevertheless, the community enthusiastically participated in SR'18 and SR'19 (Mille et al., 2018; Mille et al., 2019) as we expanded tracks to 11 languages.

This year, things look different again. There is much discussion in the field of how to control the vexed tendencies of neural generators to 'hallucinate' content (Dušek et al., 2019), and how to instil some order

Proceedings of the Third Workshop on Multilingual Surface Realisation (MSR'20), pages 1–20
Barcelona, Spain (Online), December 12, 2020.

and coherence over longer texts. Multi-hop approaches are increasingly proposed to address such issues (Hua and Wang, 2019; Zhai et al., 2019; Zhao et al., 2020), and are beginning to look somewhat like the old NLG pipeline. In this context, surface realisation is very much back on the agenda, and the term is coming back into frequent use (Zhai et al., 2019; Zhao et al., 2020). Our aim for future editions of the SR Shared Task is to test whether multi-hop gives better results overall than single-hop, but also to link up with content selection modules capable of supplying the inputs required by SR systems.

For this year, our main objective is to explore the impact of restricted vs. unrestricted resources in system training, and cross-domain generalisability. We start below with an overview of the shared task and tracks (Section 2), followed by descriptions of the participating systems (Section 3), the data (4), evaluation methods (Section 5), and results (Section 6).

2 Overview of Shared Task and Tracks

SR'20 uses the same languages and datasets as SR'19. There is a shallow and a deep track, as before; however, each track divides into two subtracks, one of which is retricted-mode, meaning only the data provided or approved for the given track may be used to train systems, the other an open track where any resources may be used in building systems. We have also created new test data sets derived from Wikipedia articles by the method described in Section 4.2 below. This year's set-up allows us to explore topline system performance and generalisability of results to a new domain.

The two main tracks are as follows:

T1 Shallow Track: The inputs in this track are UD structures in which most of the word order information has been removed and tokens have been lemmatised. In other words, it starts from unordered dependency trees with lemmatised nodes that hold PoS tags and morphological information as found in the original treebank annotations. The outputs are the fully realised sentences. The task in this track therefore amounts to determining the word order and inflecting words.

- **a. Restricted-resources subtrack (same as SR'19 Track 1)**: Teams built models trained on the provided T1 dataset(s), but use of external task-specific data was not permitted. However, teams were allowed to use external generic resources. For example, available parsers such as UUParser (Smith et al., 2018) could be run to create a silver standard versions of provided datasets and use them as additional or alternative training material. Also permitted was the use of generic publicly available off-the-shelf language models such as GPT-2 (Radford et al., 2019), ELMo (Peters et al., 2018), polyglot (Al-Rfou et al., 2013). Alternatively, BERT (Devlin et al., 2018) could be fine-tuned with publicly available datasets such as WikiText (Merity et al., 2016) or the DeepMind Q&A Dataset (Hermann et al., 2015).
- **b. Open subtrack**: In this track, teams built models trained on the provided T1 dataset(s), also using any additional resources, without restrictions. Teams could even use the SR conversion tool to produce data with the exact same specifications as the data provided in the track, by applying the converter to a parsed output (see Section 4.2).

T2 Deep Track: Inputs in this track are UD structures as in T1 from which functional words (in particular, auxiliaries, functional prepositions and conjunctions) and surface-oriented morphological and syntactic information have additionally been removed. The task in the Deep Track thus also involves introduction of functional words and morphological features, in addition to what is required for the Shallow Track.

- **a. Restricted-resources subtrack (same as SR'19 Track 2)**: Teams built models trained on the provided T2 dataset(s) using resources restricted exactly as described for T1-a above.
- **b. Open subtrack**: Teams built models trained on the provided T2 dataset(s), using additional resources without restrictions as described for T1-b above.

	2019 test sets				2020 Wiki test sets			
	T1		T2		T1		T2	
	a	b	a	b	a	b	a	b
ADAPT 20	english (ewt)	english (ewt)	–	–	english	english	–	–
BME-TUW 20	all (all)	–	–	–	all	–	–	–
Concordia 20	english (all)	–	english (all)	–	english	–	english	–
IMS 20	all (all)	all (all)	all (all)	all (all)	all	all	all	all
NILC 20	–	–	english (all)	–	–	–	english	–
BME-UW 19	*	N/A	*	N/A	all	N/A	–	N/A
IMS 19	*	N/A	*	N/A	all	N/A	all	N/A
RALI 19	–	N/A	–	N/A	english	N/A	english	N/A
Tilburg 19	–	N/A	–	N/A	all	N/A	–	N/A

Table 1: Teams submitting in each track/language (dataset); * = 2019 outputs included in human eval.

3 Participating Systems

There were two distinct sets of participating systems this year. Firstly, there were the new participants who built systems specifically for SR'20 (each system briefly summarised in Section 3.1). In addition, we asked the 2019 participants to run their systems on the new test sets, and 4 teams were able to do so (Section 3.2), two of which also submitted new systems to SR'20. Table 1 provides an overview of which teams submitted outputs in which (sub)tracks, languages and datasets. The 2019 systems can only contribute to the restricted track columns ('a') since it was the only mode of participation last year. We also indicate in the table which systems we reevaluated in the human evaluation (* in the table).

3.1 SR'20 new systems

The **ADAPT** system was trained using a custom fork of the OpenNMT-py framework, the only change made was to the beam search decoding code. The model used was a bidirectional recurrent neural network (BRNN) with long short term memory (LSTM) cells. Two variants of the ADAPT system were submitted; one trained with just the EWT dataset and one with both the EWT dataset and an augmented dataset constructed from the WikiText 103 and CNN stories corpora. (For all datasets, see Section 4.)

The **BME-TUW** system performs word order restoration by learning rules of an Interpreted Regular Tree Grammar (IRTG) that encodes the correspondence between UD-subgraphs and word orderings. The grammars build strings and UD graphs simultaneously, using pairs of operations that each connect some set of dependents to their common head while concatenating the corresponding words. The approach extends the team's 2019 system by allowing rules to reference lemmas in addition to POS-tags and by giving preference to derivations that use a smaller number of more specific rules to construct a particular UD graph. Word order restoration is performed separately for each clause. For the inflection step, a standard sequence-to-sequence model with biLSTM encoder and LSTM decoder with attention is used.

Concordia uses a text-to-text model to tackle graph-to-text surface realisation. The approach fine-tunes the pre-trained BART (Lewis et al., 2020) language model on the task of surface realisation where the model receives the linearised representation of the dependency tree and generates the surface text.

The **IMS** system builds on their system from the previous year with a substantial change in the lineariser proposed in (Yu et al., 2020), which models the task of word ordering as a Traveling Salesman Problem, and uses a biaffine attention model to calculate the bigram scores for the output sequence. To remedy the restriction of projectivity, it uses a transition system to reorder the sentence. Furthermore, model ensembling and data augmentation is applied to push the performance.

The **NILC** submission explores different ways to represent a UD structure linearly, and models the generation task by using the small version of GPT-2.

3.2 SR'19 systems run on the SR'20 new test sets

The **BME-UW** system (Kovács et al., 2019) performs word order restoration by learning Interpreted Regular Tree Grammar (IRTG) rules encoding the correspondence between UD-subgraphs and word orderings. The grammars build strings and UD graphs simultaneously, using pairs of operations each connecting a set of dependents to their common head while concatenating the corresponding words. Rule

Data type	Dataset	Track	train	dev	test
In-domain	arabic_padt (ar)	T1	6,075	909	680
	chinese_gsd (zh)	T1	3,997	500	500
	english_ewt (en)	T1, T2	12,543	2,002	2,077
	english_gum (en)	T1, T2	2,914	707	778
	english_lines (en)	T1, T2	2,738	912	914
	english_partut (en)	T1, T2	1,781	156	153
	french_gsd (fr)	T1, T2	14,450	1,476	416
	french_partut (fr)	T1, T2	803	107	110
	french_sequoia (fr)	T1, T2	2,231	412	456
	hindi_hdtb (hi)	T1	13,304	1,659	1,684
	indonesian_gsd (id)	T1	4,477	559	557
	japanese_gsd (ja)	T1	7,133	511	551
	korean_gsd (ko)	T1	4,400	950	989
	korean_kaist (ko)	T1	23,010	2,066	2,287
	portuguese_bosque (pt)	T1	8,328	560	477
	portuguese_gsd (pt)	T1	9,664	1,210	1,204
	russian_gsd (ru)	T1	3,850	579	601
	russian_syntagrus (ru)	T1	48,814	6,584	6,491
	spanish_ancora (es)	T1, T2	14,305	1,654	1,721
	spanish_gsd (es)	T1, T2	14,187	1,400	426
Out-of-domain	english_pud (en)	T1, T2	-	-	1,000
	japanese_pud (ja)	T1	-	-	1,000
	russian_pud (ru)	T1	-	-	1,000
Automatically parsed	english_ewt$_{HIT}$ (en)	T1, T2	-	-	1,795
	english_pud$_{LAT}$ (en)	T1, T2	-	-	1,032
	hindi_hdtb$_{HIT}$ (hi)	T1	-	-	1,675
	korean_kaist$_{HIT}$ (ko)	T1	-	-	2,287
	portuguese_bosque$_{STF}$ (pt)	T1	-	-	471
	spanish_ancora$_{HIT}$ (es)	T1, T2	-	-	1,723
Automatically parsed Wikipedia	english_wiki$_{STZ}$(en)	T1, T2	-	-	1,313
	french_wiki$_{STZ}$ (fr)	T1, T2	-	-	1,313
	korean_wiki$_{STZ}$ (ko)	T1	-	-	530
	portuguese_wiki$_{STZ}$ (pt)	T1	-	-	1,135
	russian_wiki$_{STZ}$ (ru)	T1	-	-	1,291
	spanish_wiki$_{STZ}$ (es)	T1, T2	-	-	1,280

Table 2: SR'20 dataset sizes for training, development and test sets (number of sentences).

weights are proportional to the observed frequency of each pattern in the training data. The inflection step uses a standard sequence-to-sequence model with biLSTM encoder and LSTM decoder with attention.

IMS (Yu et al., 2019) uses a pipeline approach for both tracks, consisting of linearisation, completion (for T2 only), inflection, and contraction. All models use the same bidirectional Tree-LSTM encoder architecture. The linearisation model orders each subtree separately with beam search, then combining the trees into a full projective tree; the completion model generates absent function words sequentially given the linearised tree of content words; the inflection model predicts a sequence of edit operations to convert lemmas to word forms character by character; the contraction model predicts BIO tags to group words to be contracted, and then generates the contracted word form of each group with a seq2seq model.

The **RALI** system (Lapalme, 2019) uses a symbolic approach to transform the dependency tree into a tree of constituents that is transformed into an English sentence by an existing English realiser, JSrealB (Molins and Lapalme, 2015). This realiser was then slightly modified for the two tracks.

The **Tilburg** approach (Ferreira and Krahmer, 2019), based on Ferreira et al. (2018), realises texts by first preprocessing the dependency tree into a preordered linearized form, which is then converted into its textual counterpart using a rule-based approach together with a statistical machine translation (SMT) model. A singular version of the model was trained for each language considered in the experiment.

4 Data Sets

4.1 T1 and T2 training and test sets (same as in SR'19)

There are 42 datasets in 11 languages, 29 datasets for T1, and 13 for T2 (for a summary overview, see Table 2, top 3 sections of the table). The datasets were selected from the available collection of

Language	Dataset	Performance (LAS)	Performance (lemmas)	Best CoNLL'18 (LAS)	Best CoNLL'18 (lemmas)
English	ewt	83.59	97.21	84.57	97.23
French	gsd	89.05	97.64	86.89	97.03
Korean	gsd	83.53	92.69	85.14	94.02
Portuguese	bosque	87.57	97.8	87.81	97.54
Russian	syntagrus	90.06	97.51	92.48	98.19
Spanish	ancora	90.01	99.19	90.93	99.02

Table 3: Datasets used to train the Stanza parsing models.

UD datasets mainly based on the completeness of annotations in terms of PoS tags and morphologically relevant markup (number, tense, verbal finiteness, etc.). The test data sets can be grouped into three types: (i) in-domain test data, in the same domains as the training and development data; (ii) Out-of-domain, which are test sets of parallel sentences in different languages in domains not covered by the training and development data; and (iii) silver standard data, which consists of automatically parsed sentences.

The in-domain and out-of-domain data is provided in the UD release V2.3.[1] The silver standard data was processed using the best CoNLL'18 parsers for the chosen datasets: the Harbin HIT-SCIR (*HIT*) parser (Che et al., 2017) for English_ewt, Hindi_hdtb, Korean_kaist and Spanish_ancora; the LATTICE (*LAT*) parser (Lim et al., 2018) for English_pud and the Stanford (*STF*) parser (Qi et al., 2019) for Portuguese_bosque.[2] A detailed description of all SR'19 datasets and how they were processed can be found in the SR'19 report paper (Mille et al., 2019).

4.2 SR'20 new test sets

To obtain new test sets,[3] we selected sentences from Wikipedia in six out of the eleven SR'19 languages for which it was possible to get a good quantity of clean texts on the same topics. The used articles contain mostly landmarks and some historical figures. On the extracted sentences, we applied extensive filtering to achieve reasonably good text quality. We skipped sentences that include special characters, contain unusual tokens (e.g. ISBN), or have unbalanced quotation marks or brackets. Furthermore, we took only sentences with more than 5 tokens and shorter than 50 tokens. After the initial filtering, quite a few malformed sentences remained. In order to remove those, we scored the sentences with BERT and kept only the best scored half. Finally, via manual inspection we identified patterns and expressions to reduce the number of malformed sentences still further.

We parsed the cleaned Wikipedia sentences with the Stanza parser (Qi et al., 2020), using the trained models provided for the respective languages; the Stanza parser gets very competitive results on a large set of languages (see Table 3). For each language, we executed the parser with the processors for Tokenisation and Sentence Split, Multi-word Token Expansion, Part-of-Speech and Morphological Tagging, Lemmatisation and Dependency Parsing. The performance of the parser for all six languages in terms of Labelled Attachment Score and lemmatisation, two of the crucial aspects for our task, is provided in Table 3; for reference, we also provide the LAS and lemma scores of the best parser on each dataset according to the CoNLL'18 shared task results. All the datasets and their respective sizes are summarised in Table 2; the *STZ* extension in the last 6 rows of the table indicate a reference to the Stanza parser.

As it was the case in the previous editions of the task, Shallow Track inputs were generated with the aid of Python scripts from the UD structures, using all available input sentences (inflected forms and most word order information are removed), and Deep Track inputs were then generated by automatically processing the Shallow Track structures using a series of graph-transduction grammars for removing functional nodes and other superficial features, and generalising the dependency relations; see SR'19 report (Mille et al., 2019) for details. The code for converting the UD trees into SR'19/SR'20 Shallow

[1] `https://universaldependencies.org/`

[2] The CoNLL'18 shared task submissions were downloaded from `https://lindat.mff.cuni.cz/repository/xmlui/handle/11234/1-2885`.

[3] The complete SR'20 datasets can be downloaded from `https://sites.google.com/site/genchalrepository/surface-realisation/sr-20-multilingual`

1	Will	will	AUX	MD	VerbForm=Fin	6	aux
2	it	it	PRON	PRP	Case=Nom|Gender=Neut|Number=Sing|Person=3|PronType=Prs	6	nsubj
3	not	not	PART	RB	_	6	advmod
4	also	also	ADV	RB	_	6	advmod
5	be	be	AUX	VB	VerbForm=Inf	6	cop
6	grandiose	grandiose	ADJ	JJ	Degree=Pos	0	root
7	in	in	ADP	IN	_	9	case
8	its	its	PRON	PRP$	Gender=Neut|Number=Sing|Person=3|Poss=Yes|PronType=Prs	9	nmod:poss
9	way	way	NOUN	NN	Number=Sing	6	obl
10	?	?	PUNCT	.	_	6	punct

Figure 1: Sample UD structure (without the last two columns).

1	not	_	PART	RB	_	10	advmod
2	its	_	PRON	PRP$	Gender=Neut|Number=Sing|Person=3|Poss=Yes|PronType=Prs	7	nmod:poss
3	?	_	PUNCT	.	lin=+1	10	punct
4	be	_	AUX	VB	VerbForm=Inf	10	cop
5	it	_	PRON	PRP	Case=Nom|Gender=Neut|Number=Sing|Person=3|PronType=Prs	10	nsubj
6	also	_	ADV	RB	_	10	advmod
7	way	_	NOUN	NN	Number=Sing	10	obl
8	in	_	ADP	IN	_	7	case
9	will	_	AUX	MD	VerbForm=Fin	10	aux
10	grandiose	_	ADJ	JJ	Degree=Pos	0	root

Figure 2: Sample T1 input structure (without the last two columns).

1	not	_	PART	_	_	2	A1INV
2	grandiose	_	ADJ	_	Tense=Fut|Degree=Pos|ClauseType=Int	0	ROOT
3	it	_	PRON	_	Number=Sing|Person=3|PronType=Prs	2	A1
4	also	_	ADV	_	_	2	A1INV
5	way	_	NOUN	_	Number=Sing	2	AM
6	its	_	PRON	_	Number=Sing|Poss=Yes|Person=3|PronType=Prs	5	AM

Figure 3: Sample T2 input structure (without the last two columns).

and Deep Track inputs is available on GitLab.[4] Figures 1, 2 and 3 shown sample UD, Track 1 and Track 2 structures respectively, taken from the parsed Wikipedia English dataset.

5 Evaluation Methods

5.1 Automatic methods

We used BLEU, NIST, BERT, and inverse normalised character-based string-edit distance (referred to as DIST, for short, below) to assess submitted systems. BLEU (Papineni et al., 2002) is a precision metric that computes the geometric mean of the n-gram precisions between generated text and reference texts and adds a brevity penalty for shorter sentences. We use the smoothed version and report results for $n = 4$. NIST[5] is a related n-gram similarity metric weighted in favor of less frequent n-grams which are taken to be more informative. DIST starts by computing the minimum number of character inserts, deletes and substitutions (all at cost 1) required to turn the system output into the (single) reference text. The resulting number is then divided by the number of characters in the reference text, and finally subtracted from 1, in order to align with the other metrics. Spaces and punctuation marks count as characters; output texts were otherwise normalised as for all metrics (see below). BERTScore (Zhang et al., 2020) computes a token-based similarity score by comparing each token of the generated texts with each token of the reference sentence. BERTScore uses contextual embeddings rather than exact matches, and has been shown to correlate better with human judgments than other commonly used metrics. The figures in the tables below are the system-level scores for BLEU, NIST and BERTScore, and the mean sentence-level scores for DIST.

Output texts were normalised prior to computing metrics by lower-casing all tokens, removing any extraneous whitespace characters. Missing outputs were scored 0. We only report results for all sentences (incorporating the missing-output penalty), rather than also separately reporting scores for just the in-coverage items.

[4] https://gitlab.com/talnupf/ud2deep

[5] http://www.itl.nist.gov/iad/mig/tests/mt/doc/ngram-study.pdf; http://www.itl.nist.gov/iad/mig/tests/mt/2009/

5.2 Human-assessed methods

For the human evaluation, we selected a subset of language/dataset combinations based on number of submissions received and availability of evaluators: three in-domain datasets (English_ewt, Russian_syntagrus, Spanish_ancora), and the three corresponding Wikipedia datasets for these languages. All submitted Track 1 and Track 2 outputs for these datasets were evaluated, plus two 2019 outputs (IMS, BME-UW) for each in-domain dataset, which were already evaluated in 2019.

We adopted the same approach to human evaluation as in SR'18 (Mille et al., 2018) and SR'19 (Mille et al., 2019). The evaluation method is Direct Assessment (DA) (Graham et al., 2016), as used by the WMT competitions to produce the official ranking of machine translation systems (Barrault et al., 2020) and video captioning systems at TRECvid (Graham et al., 2018; Awad et al., 2019). We ran the evaluation on Mechanical Turk,[6] assessing two quality criteria, in separate evaluation experiments, but using the same method: *Readability* and *Meaning Similarity*. We used continuous sliders as rating tools, the evidence being that raters tend to prefer them (Belz and Kow, 2011). Slider positions were mapped to values from 0 to 100 (best).

Raters were given brief instructions, including the direction to ignore formatting errors, superfluous whitespace, capitalisation issues, and poor hyphenation. The statement to be assessed in the Readability evaluation was: *The text reads well and is free from grammatical errors and awkward constructions.*

The corresponding statement in the Meaning Similarity evaluation, in which system outputs ('the black text') were compared to reference sentences ('the gray text'), was:[7,8] *The meaning of the gray text is adequately expressed by the black text.*

The DA method involves quality assurance techniques as follows. System outputs are randomly assigned to HITs (following Mechanical Turk terminology) of 100 outputs, of which 20 are used solely for quality assurance (QA) (i.e. do not count towards system scores): (i) some are repeated as-is, (ii) some are repeated in a 'damaged' version and (iii) some are replaced by their corresponding reference texts. In each case, a minimum threshold has to be reached for the HIT to be accepted: for (i), scores must be similar enough, for (ii) the score for the damaged version must be worse, and for (iii) the score for the reference text must be high. For full details of how these additional texts are created and thresholds applied, please refer to Barrault et al. (2019). We report QA figures for the MTurk evaluations below.

Test set sizes out of the box varied for the different languages. For the human test sets we selected a subset of at least 500 sentences for each language, motivated by the power analysis provided by Graham et al. (2019). For subsets, test set items were selected randomly.

We follow the same format for reporting results as WMT adopt when reporting DA method results, i.e. we report both average raw scores and average standardised scores per system in the tabular form shown in the results tables below. In order to produce standardised scores we simply map each individual evaluator's scores to their standard scores (or z-scores) computed on the set of all raw scores by the given evaluator using each evaluator's mean and standard deviation. For both raw and standard scores, we compute the mean of sentence-level scores.

6 Results

In this section, we present evaluation results produced with all evaluation methods from the preceding section, for all test set outputs received from participants. The best scores are generally better this year compared to 2019, both according to automatically computed metrics and human assessments. By way of introduction, Table 4 shows a sample output for one of the English Wikipedia sentences, as generated by each participating system. T1 and T2 inputs for these sample outputs are shown above in Figures 2 and 3 respectively. Interestingly, the outputs show a lot of variation, and none of them gets the target exactly. The last column shows the percentage of sentences exactly matching their human-written reference for each system, as calculated on the English_wiki dataset (1,313 sentences).

[6]We were able to reuse, with minor adaptations, the code produced for the WMT'17 evaluations: `https://github.com/ygraham/segment-mteval`

[7]Since a main proportion of workers on Mechanical Turk are located in the US, we employ US spelling in evaluations.

[8]Past work in machine translation has investigated the degree to which the presence of a reference sentence might introduce

System	Sample output	Exact (%)
HUMAN	Will it not also be grandiose in its way?	
ADAPT20aT1	In its way it will alson't be grandiose?	15.8
ADAPT20bT1	Will it also not be grandiose in its way?	27.11
BME19T1	It will also be not grandiose in its way ?	0.57
BME20aT1	Also be it will not grandiose in its way ?	0.57
Concordia20aT1	Will it also not be grandiose in its way ?	0.46
Concordia20aT2	It will also not be grandiose in its way .	0.42
IMS19T1	Will not it also be grandiose in its way?	16.41
IMS19T2	It should also not grandiose in its way?	1.18
IMS20aT1	It will not be also grandiose in its way?	18.74
IMS20aT2	It will also not be grandiose in its way?	1.56
IMS20bT1	It will also not be grandiose in its way?	21.59
IMS20bT2	Will it also not be grandiose in its way?	2.17
NILC20aT2	It will also be n't in its way;	1.56
RALI19T1	It? will not be grandiose also in its way.	0.46
RALI19T2	It is grandiose not also its way.	0.46
Tilburg19T1	it will also be not grandiose in its way.	0.23

Table 4: Sample system outputs for the inputs in Figures 2 and 3, and % of exact matches on English_wiki (systems in alphabetical order).

6.1 Automatic Evaluation Results

6.1.1 Overview and of metric results provided

Tables 5, 6, 7, 8, 9, 10, 11 and 12 show the results of the automatic evaluations with BLEU, NIST, DIST, and BERTScore on all test sets. We have grouped results tables together by metric, so that the first page of results shows all BLEU results, in Tables 5 and 6; the second page of results shows all NIST results, in Tables 7 and 8; the third page of results shows all DIST results, in Tables 9 and 10; and the fourth page shows all BERT results, in Tables 11 and 12. In each case, the first, larger, table shows results for the 2019 test sets, whereas the second, smaller table shows results for the new 2020 Wikipedia test sets. In each table, the column headings show the system team, system year (20, 19) and subtrack (a, b) for which results are shown in a column, while the row labels in the first column show which test set and track (T1, T2) results are for. Rows are shown in alphabetical order of the test set name (ar_padt, en_ewt, etc.). For an overview of test sets, see Table 2.

In Section 6.3, we furthermore provide comparisons between automatic and human evaluations.

6.1.2 Discussion of metric results

Considering all metric results tables together, scores are generally (but not always) higher for 2020 systems than for comparable 2019 systems (e.g. BLEU for **BME20a** is higher for most test sets than for **BME19**, Table 5); and T1 results are higher in all cases than directly comparable T2 results. The picture for 'a' subtracks (restricted) compared to 'b' subtracks (unrestricted) is different. Here we have two teams who submitted comparable outputs for both subtracks, **ADAPT** and **IMS**. **ADAPT** submitted just for T1 en_ewt, and here, all results for 'b' are higher than comparable results for 'a'. **IMS** submitted for all datasets in both subtracks 'a' and 'b' in both T1 and T2. For the 2019 tests, the picture is mixed, and there is no clear, consistent benefit from additional resources. However, for the 2020 out-of-domain Wikipedia test sets, 'b' scores are always greater than (or in one case equal to) comparable 'b' scores, with the margin bigger for T2 scores than T1.

Taking a closer look at improvements this year compared to 2019, we see for instance, on the **English_ewt** test set, last year's top BLEU score in T1 (the Shallow Track) was 82.98 (**IMS**); in 2020, it goes up to 86.16 in the restricted track (**IMS**), and 87.5 in the open track (**ADAPT**). In T2 (the Deep Track), top BLEU scores also increased, from 54.75 (**IMS**) to 58.84 in the restricted track, and 58.66 in the unrestricted track (both **IMS**).

We next look at overall improvements of team submissions across all test sets they submitted outputs

bias into the evaluation revealing no significant evidence of reference-bias (Ma et al., 2017).

-BLEU-4-	ADAPT		BME		Concordia	IMS			NILC
	20a	20b	20a	19	20a	20a	20b	19	20a
T1_ar_padt			26	26.4		69.56	69.71	64.9	
T1_en_ewt	80.4	87.5	57.25	59.22	70.71	86.16	85.67	82.98	
T2_en_ewt					58.44	58.84	58.66	54.75	45.19
T1_en_gum			60.77	57.57	66.98	88.89	89.7	83.84	
T2_en_gum					53.92	53.98	56.33	52.45	40.94
T1_en_lines			55.98	48.78	62.7	85.05	85.3	81	
T2_en_lines					47.96	50.23	50.45	47.29	41.04
T1_en_partut			57.96	61.37	67.05	89.72	89.37	87.25	
T2_en_partut					50.54	46.87	50.11	45.89	43.41
T1_es_ancora			59.32	61.09		87.42	87.34	83.7	
T2_es_ancora						56.67	55.64	53.13	
T1_es_gsd			54.6	53.74		84.61	84.52	82.98	
T2_es_gsd						55.1	55.99	51.17	
T1_fr_gsd			43.21	43.8		86.08	85.08	84	
T2_fr_gsd						58.86	56.95	53.62	
T1_fr_partut			52.46	49.17		87.09	89.22	83.38	
T2_fr_partut						51.11	57.62	46.95	
T1_fr_sequoia			45.25	46.72		87.25	87.29	85.01	
T2_fr_sequoia						59.37	60.26	57.41	
T1_hi_hdtb			57.2	63.63		84.53	84.77	80.56	
T1_id_gsd			59.16	54.22		87.53	88.33	85.34	
T1_ja_gsd			50.89	49.53		89.36	89.54	87.69	
T1_ko_gsd			58.37	46.08		81.14	82.52	74.19	
T1_ko_kaist			57.05	47.23		79.96	80.28	73.93	
T1_pt_bosque			39.89	39.53		82.92	83.36	77.75	
T1_pt_gsd			30.68	30.39		80.59	80.69	75.93	
T1_ru_gsd			54.28	54.58		77.43	78.93	71.23	
T1_ru_syntagrus			54.79	50.91		81.82	79.78	76.95	
T1_zh_gsd			50.58	58.72		86.36	88.05	83.85	
T1_en_pud			58.67	60.42	74.47	85.37	85.65	86.61	
T2_en_pud					58.45	50.59	53.7	51.01	42.6
T1_ja_pud			51.08	53.65		88.88	89.21	86.64	
T1_ru_pud			46.07	10.15		69.07	69.35	58.38	
T1_en_ewt$_{HIT}$			55.5	58.07	67.12	84.72	84.31	81.8	
T2_en_ewt$_{HIT}$					56.01	57.1	57.14	53.54	43.15
T1_en_pud$_{LAT}$			54.76	53.46	73.41	79.74	80.14	82.6	
T2_en_pud$_{LAT}$					56.69	47.96	50.15	47.6	42.64
T1_es_ancora$_{HIT}$			59.7	61.26		86.97	86.81	83.31	
T2_es_ancora$_{HIT}$						56.92	55.96	53.54	
T1_hi_hdtb$_{HIT}$			56.83	64.27		84.42	84.78	80.19	
T1_ko_kaist$_{HIT}$			56.74	46.72		81.01	81.42	74.27	
T1_pt_bosque$_{STA}$			41.86	40.42		84.35	85.18	78.97	
Macro-avg	80.4	87.5	51.96	50.04	61.75	74.56	75.13	71.13	42.71

Table 5: BLEU scores on the 2019 datasets, with indicative average scores on the submitted outputs.

-BLEU-4-	ADAPT		BME		Concordia	IMS			NILC	RALI	Tilburg
	20a	20b	20a	19	20a	20a	20b	19	20a	19	19
T1_en_wiki$_{STZ}$	84.11	94.32	60.8	63.37	74.66	88.34	90.85	86.54		43.73	61.54
T2_en_wiki$_{STZ}$					57.49	52.8	56.26	49.74	39.68	25.23	
T1_es_wiki$_{STZ}$			61.13	16.34		87.85	88.28	84.97			58.18
T2_es_wiki$_{STZ}$						52.86	56.19	51.69			
T1_fr_wiki$_{STZ}$			46.33	51.14		89.22	90.6	87.79			56.59
T2_fr_wiki$_{STZ}$						59.22	60.68	55.74			
T1_ko_wiki$_{STZ}$			53.61	40.9		76.57	81.65	73.81			1.72
T1_pt_wiki$_{STZ}$			42.22	11.78		83.57	84.74	79.69			36.88
T1_ru_wiki$_{STZ}$			51.89	13.54		77.91	76.31	73.86			34.01
Macro-avg	84.11	94.32	52.66	32.85	66.08	74.26	76.17	71.54	39.68	34.48	41.49

Table 6: BLEU scores on the Wikipedia datasets, with indicative average scores on the submitted outputs.

–NIST–	ADAPT		BME		Concordia	IMS			NILC
	20a	20b	20a	19	20a	20a	20b	19	20a
T1_ar_padt			8.29	8.29		12.63	12.62	12.22	
T1_en_ewt	13.47	13.81	12.52	12.62	12.7	13.78	13.74	13.61	
T2_en_ewt					11.61	12.13	12.14	11.79	9.96
T1_en_gum			12.1	11.99	11.62	12.96	12.98	12.69	
T2_en_gum					10.51	11.09	11.25	11.04	9
T1_en_lines			11.78	11.54	11.3	12.98	12.97	12.71	
T2_en_lines					9.93	10.82	10.89	10.63	9.09
T1_en_partut			10.22	10.34	9.83	11.07	11.05	11.01	
T2_en_partut					8.57	8.92	9.26	9.03	8.24
T1_es_ancora			13.57	13.52		14.9	14.89	14.69	
T2_es_ancora						12.66	12.66	12.38	
T1_es_gsd			11.6	11.44		12.86	12.86	12.77	
T2_es_gsd						11.05	11.13	10.82	
T1_fr_gsd			10.41	10.33		12.58	12.55	12.45	
T2_fr_gsd						11.14	11.06	10.79	
T1_fr_partut			9.05	8.99		10.56	10.58	10.36	
T2_fr_partut						8.38	8.88	8.27	
T1_fr_sequoia			10.56	10.55		12.65	12.64	12.53	
T2_fr_sequoia						11.02	11.21	11	
T1_hi_hdtb			11.98	12.26		13.32	13.34	13.07	
T1_id_gsd			12.14	11.82		12.89	12.91	12.83	
T1_ja_gsd			10.08	9.99		12.53	12.54	12.42	
T1_ko_gsd			12.12	11.98		12.44	12.46	12.27	
T1_ko_kaist			12.77	12.65		13.18	13.19	13	
T1_pt_bosque			9.89	9.77		12.4	12.41	12.15	
T1_pt_gsd			8.97	8.85		13.33	13.34	13.07	
T1_ru_gsd			11.9	11.91		12.4	12.42	12.15	
T1_ru_syntagrus			14.17	13.8		15.45	15.34	15.08	
T1_zh_gsd			11.62	11.85		12.86	12.91	12.78	
T1_en_pud			12.48	12.6	12.62	13.41	13.41	13.47	
T2_en_pud					11.43	11.36	11.59	11.45	9.68
T1_ja_pud			10.34	10.56		13.2	13.23	13.02	
T1_ru_pud			11.26	9.64		11.85	11.89	10.91	
T1_en_ewt$_{HIT}$			12.36	12.49	12.4	13.61	13.59	13.46	
T2_en_ewt$_{HIT}$					11.19	11.88	11.92	11.55	9.64
T1_en_pud$_{LAT}$			12.27	12.29	12.52	13.16	13.16	13.26	
T2_en_pud$_{LAT}$					11.18	11.02	11.19	11.08	9.59
T1_es_ancora$_{HIT}$			13.57	13.51		14.81	14.8	14.61	
T2_es_ancora$_{HIT}$						12.63	12.63	12.36	
T1_hi_hdtb$_{HIT}$			11.97	12.29		13.31	13.33	13.05	
T1_ko_kaist$_{HIT}$			12.77	12.63		13.22	13.23	13.02	
T1_pt_bosque$_{STA}$			9.89	9.73		12.4	12.43	12.14	
Macro-avg	13.47	13.81	11.47	11.39	11.24	12.4	12.44	12.21	9.31

Table 7: NIST scores on the 2019 datasets, with indicative average scores on the submitted outputs.

–NIST–	ADAPT		BME		Concordia	IMS			NILC	RALI	Tilburg
	20a	20b	20a	19	20a	20a	20b	19	20a	19	19
T1_en_wiki$_{STZ}$	13.77	14.3	12.76	12.94	12.9	14	14.14	13.91		10.99	12.72
T2_en_wiki$_{STZ}$					11.57	11.82	12.12	11.56	9.31	8.74	
T1_es_wiki$_{STZ}$			13.03	10.5		14.09	14.1	13.95			12.81
T2_es_wiki$_{STZ}$						11.72	12.04	11.22			
T1_fr_wiki$_{STZ}$			11.25	11.42		13.98	14.09	14			12.04
T2_fr_wiki$_{STZ}$						12.06	12.28	11.72			
T1_ko_wiki$_{STZ}$			11.12	10.98		11.5	11.55	11.37			3.24
T1_pt_wiki$_{STZ}$			10.64	9.26		13.57	13.61	13.25			9.61
T1_ru_wiki$_{STZ}$			12.04	10.87		12.86	12.86	12.65			10.04
Macro-avg	13.77	14.3	11.81	11	12.24	12.84	12.98	12.63	9.31	9.87	10.08

Table 8: NIST scores on the Wikipedia datasets, with indicative average scores on the submitted outputs.

–DIST–	ADAPT		BME		Concordia	IMS			NILC
	20a	20b	20a	19	20a	20a	20b	19	20a
T1_ar_padt			44.78	43.06		75.8	76.51	73.71	
T1_en_ewt	85.5	90.35	65.23	62.69	77.94	88.48	87.74	86.72	
T2_en_ewt					73.66	78.99	79.23	76.3	64.83
T1_en_gum			62.86	56.07	69.87	91.41	91.97	83.49	
T2_en_gum					67.02	73.22	76.47	73.07	60.42
T1_en_lines			61.44	52.77	68.62	85.89	86.48	82.21	
T2_en_lines					64.33	73.06	73.1	71.93	61.18
T1_en_partut			58.39	61.22	71.59	90.38	88.73	85.68	
T2_en_partut					62.39	69.75	72.98	67.45	59.74
T1_es_ancora			55.66	58.15		85.66	85.26	79.82	
T2_es_ancora						71.85	71.52	68.58	
T1_es_gsd			55.5	59.03		82.6	82.53	79.45	
T2_es_gsd						71.01	72.53	68.85	
T1_fr_gsd			55.48	59.35		84.64	83.24	84.15	
T2_fr_gsd						72.38	71.94	68.82	
T1_fr_partut			62.26	56.87		85.84	87.67	82.32	
T2_fr_partut						68.43	75.04	68.99	
T1_fr_sequoia			57.61	59.28		85.65	85.12	85.13	
T2_fr_sequoia						73.71	73.3	72.06	
T1_hi_hdtb			57.55	64.04		83.03	83.14	79.07	
T1_id_gsd			59.62	55.57		86.41	87.11	83.92	
T1_ja_gsd			60.57	57.03		87	87.83	87.17	
T1_ko_gsd			66.14	52.1		85.49	86.82	80.95	
T1_ko_kaist			62.88	50.9		84.52	84.9	78.69	
T1_pt_bosque			55.63	58.72		84.59	85.45	79.8	
T1_pt_gsd			53.49	54.93		87.86	87.7	79.33	
T1_ru_gsd			53.78	52.67		78.89	81.54	73.04	
T1_ru_syntagrus			56.72	55.6		83.02	81.07	78.66	
T1_zh_gsd			54.56	59.29		83.89	85.19	83.18	
T1_en_pud			61.85	59.84	76.46	85.75	84.52	87	
T2_en_pud					68.83	70.43	73.31	72.31	59.85
T1_ja_pud			55.77	56.72		85.67	86.29	84.04	
T1_ru_pud			56.17	32.08		82.4	82.67	77.12	
T1_en_ewt$_{HIT}$			62.82	60.36	74.47	86.65	86.24	85.35	
T2_en_ewt$_{HIT}$					69	77.23	76.98	74.99	62.2
T1_en_pud$_{LAT}$			59.93	56.13	77.68	82.19	82.23	86.18	
T2_en_pud$_{LAT}$					67.79	70.53	72.76	71.65	60.43
T1_es_ancora$_{HIT}$			56.14	58.38		86.96	86.36	81.14	
T2_es_ancora$_{HIT}$						73.27	73.06	70.02	
T1_hi_hdtb$_{HIT}$			57.43	64.58		83.52	84.05	78.88	
T1_ko_kaist$_{HIT}$			62.31	50.16		85.36	85.82	79.12	
T1_pt_bosque$_{STA}$			56.6	59.72		87.35	87.98	81.56	
Macro-avg	85.5	90.35	58.25	56.11	70.69	81.21	81.77	78.38	61.24

Table 9: DIST scores on the 2019 datasets, with indicative average scores on the submitted outputs.

–DIST–	ADAPT		BME		Concordia	IMS			NILC	RALI	Tilburg
	20a	20b	20a	19	20a	20a	20b	19	20a	19	19
T1_en_wiki$_{STZ}$	84.93	94.56	62.73	60.94	76.93	86.51	89.21	86.52		58.42	71.69
T2_en_wiki$_{STZ}$					67.26	72.53	74.94	71.46	57.56	50.68	
T1_es_wiki$_{STZ}$			57.66	35.26		87.35	87.68	81.39			63.27
T2_es_wiki$_{STZ}$						73.5	75.84	71.46			
T1_fr_wiki$_{STZ}$			58.82	66.53		91.64	92.58	86.44			70.12
T2_fr_wiki$_{STZ}$						73.68	76.64	72.53			
T1_ko_wiki$_{STZ}$			62.55	49.04		80.2	85.99	79.87			47.12
T1_pt_wiki$_{STZ}$			59.08	34.89		84.58	86.4	81.54			62.93
T1_ru_wiki$_{STZ}$			56.67	33.07		82.37	80.09	77.26			55.85
Macro-avg	84.93	94.56	59.59	46.62	72.1	81.37	83.26	78.72	57.56	54.55	61.83

Table 10: DIST scores on the Wikipedia datasets, with indicative average scores on the submitted outputs.

-**BERT**-	ADAPT		BME		Concordia	IMS			NILC
	20a	20b	20a	19	20a	20a	20b	19	20a
T1_ar_padt			0.9595	0.9618		0.9835	0.9836	0.9812	
T1_en_ewt	0.9815	0.9924	0.9473	0.958	0.9565	0.9849	0.9844	0.9819	
T2_en_ewt					0.9635	0.965	0.9643	0.9607	0.941 1
T1_en_gum			0.943	0.9503	0.9555	0.9897	0.9904	0.9829	
T2_en_gum					0.9572	0.9586	0.9624	0.9573	0.939 9
T1_en_lines			0.9341	0.9321	0.9565	0.9819	0.9826	0.9765	
T2_en_lines					0.9487	0.9519	0.9535	0.9491	0.938 1
T1_en_partut			0.934	0.9474	0.9565	0.9857	0.985	0.9829	
T2_en_partut					0.9505	0.9464	0.9528	0.9433	0.943 8
T1_es_ancora			0.9509	0.9612		0.9893	0.9891	0.9843	
T2_es_ancora						0.9644	0.9642	0.9601	
T1_es_gsd			0.9498	0.9584		0.9743	0.9738	0.9798	
T2_es_gsd						0.9532	0.9545	0.9561	
T1_fr_gsd			0.9414	0.9584		0.9853	0.9845	0.9835	
T2_fr_gsd						0.964	0.9622	0.9583	
T1_fr_partut			0.9452	0.9501		0.9886	0.9902	0.9854	
T2_fr_partut						0.954	0.9649	0.9525	
T1_fr_sequoia			0.9452	0.9562		0.9869	0.9872	0.9857	
T2_fr_sequoia						0.966	0.9666	0.9629	
T1_hi_hdtb			0.9808	0.9836		0.992	0.992	0.99	
T1_id_gsd			0.9589	0.9581		0.9707	0.9708	0.9843	
T1_ja_gsd			0.8833	0.9679		0.9917	0.9921	0.9914	
T1_ko_gsd			0.9814	0.9784		0.9933	0.9936	0.9903	
T1_ko_kaist			0.9811	0.976		0.9919	0.9921	0.9887	
T1_pt_bosque			0.9463	0.9546		0.9856	0.9857	0.98	
T1_pt_gsd			0.9297	0.9374		0.9845	0.9844	0.9785	
T1_ru_gsd			0.9702	0.9755		0.7624	0.7626	0.9828	
T1_ru_syntagrus			0.9718	0.9769		0.991	0.9899	0.9882	
T1_zh_gsd			0.887	0.9688		0.9894	0.9906	0.9884	
T1_en_pud			0.9385	0.9482	0.9605	0.9812	0.9812	0.983	
T2_en_pud					0.9613	0.9515	0.9557	0.9607	0.938 2
T1_ja_pud			0.8761	0.9666		0.9905	0.9909	0.9892	
T1_ru_pud			0.9686	0.9612		0.9876	0.9878	0.9833	
T1_en_ewt$_{HIT}$			0.9431	0.9535	0.9562	0.9824	0.982	0.9806	
T2_en_ewt$_{HIT}$					0.9593	0.9614	0.9611	0.9578	0.939 2
T1_en_pud$_{LAT}$			0.9333	0.9383	0.9596	0.9734	0.9738	0.9785	
T2_en_pud$_{LAT}$					0.9584	0.9475	0.9505	0.9474	0.936 8
T1_es_ancora$_{HIT}$			0.9506	0.9607		0.9886	0.988	0.9843	
T2_es_ancora$_{HIT}$						0.9641	0.9636	0.9601	
T1_hi_hdtb$_{HIT}$			0.9806	0.984		0.9922	0.9923	0.9898	
T1_ko_kaist$_{HIT}$			0.9768	0.9757		0.9924	0.9927	0.9892	
T1_pt_bosque$_{STA}$			0.9475	0.9544		0.9856	0.9868	0.9795	
Macro-avg	0.9815	0.9924	0.9468	0.9605	0.9572	0.972	0.9728	0.9755	0.9396

Table 11: BERT scores on the 2019 datasets, with indicative average scores on the submitted outputs.

-**BERT**-	ADAPT		BME		Concordia	IMS			NILC	RALI	Tilburg
	20a	20b	20a	19	20a	20a	20b	19	20a	19	19
T1_en_wiki$_{STZ}$	0.9826	0.9849	0.9413	0.9435	0.9614	0.9856	0.9882	0.9837		0.9396	0.938
T2_en_wiki$_{STZ}$					0.9473	0.9555	0.959	0.9515	0.9317	0.9171	
T1_es_wiki$_{STZ}$			0.952	0.9089		0.9893	0.9892	0.9853			0.9477
T2_es_wiki$_{STZ}$						0.9638	0.9671	0.9613			
T1_fr_wiki$_{STZ}$			0.9435	0.9508		0.9902	0.9917	0.9872			0.9512
T2_fr_wiki$_{STZ}$						0.9637	0.9667	0.9606			
T1_ko_wiki$_{STZ}$			0.9756	0.9683		0.9895	0.9919	0.9612			0.9354
T1_pt_wiki$_{STZ}$			0.948	0.9107		0.9801	0.9857	0.9801			0.9385
T1_ru_wiki$_{STZ}$			0.9707	0.9604		0.9883	0.987	0.986			0.9645
Macro-avg	0.9826	0.9849	0.9552	0.9404	0.9826	0.9784	0.9807	0.973	0.9317	0.9284	0.9459

Table 12: BERT scores on the Wikipedia datasets, with indicative average scores on the submitted outputs.

for, which we roughly approximate with macro-averages of all scores for a given metric as indicated in the bottom row of each metric results table. **BME-UW** and **IMS** improved their 2019 average scores on all datasets by 1.92 and 3.43 BLEU points respectively (+4 points in the open track for **IMS**), while **ADAPT** increased its score by 0.7 BLEU points, and almost 8 points in the open track. **Concordia** substantially improved their system compared to last year, now generating also from T2 inputs, and obtaining the highest BLEU scores on half of the English T2 datasets.

We now turn to comparisons between results for gold standard annotated datasets, and datasets with automatically generated inputs (silver standard data), for the same language. As in 2019, for the English and Spanish gold standards datasets (ewt and ancora), systems score equally high or higher than on the silver standard datasets (pred$_{HIT}$) for the same language; this year this is also true for Korean and Hindi, but not for Portuguese. On the new 2020 datasets, all of which are silver standard (see Section 4.2), the general tendency is that systems score higher than on the gold standard datasets (this is the case for 6 out of 9 test sets), even for systems that were not further developed compared to last year (**BME-UW**, **RALI**, **Tilburg**).[9] For 2 of the 9 Wikipedia datasets, namely Korean and Russian, all systems score lower than on any 2019 dataset in the same language, and on English-T2, only a few scores are higher than on the 2019 silver-standard datasets (but never higher than on the gold standard datasets). One explanation to the generally higher scores on the Wikipedia datasets might be that these contain cleaner sentences, or at least sentences are easier to parse and generate from, than those in the other data sets, which contain more varied and less standard sentences.

In terms of highest scores, bearing in mind scores aren't directly comparable across different test sets, we note that stand-out highest scores were achieved on the new 2020 Wikipedia English dataset in T1 by **ADAPT** which reaches over 94 BLEU / 14.3 NIST / 94 DIST, in subtrack 'b' (unrestricted resources). **IMS** matches this performance in terms of BERT score only. **IMS** also has the highest scores on all other new 2020 Wikipedia test sets in terms of all metrics (in some cases being the only team that submitted), except for the T2_en_wiki 'b' BLEU score, where **Concordia** reaches 57.49. As mentioned in the human evaluation section, **ADAPT**'s very high scores on T2_en_wiki 'b' subtrack are in part due to the fact that it used models trained on WikiText-103 (Merity et al., 2016).

6.2 Human Evaluation Results

Tables 13 and 14 show results from the human evaluations with Direct Assessment (DA) for English, Russian and Spanish (see Section 5.2 for details of the evaluation method). The datasets included were as shown in the results tables, and included all new SR'20 test sets. For each dataset, system outputs in the Shallow (T1) and Deep (T2) Tracks were evaluated in the same experiment.

Results from DA quality control were as follows. A total of 183,000 human assessments were collected on Mturk.[10] A lower rate of bad data was incurred with a higher proportion of Mturk workers, 48% passing quality control, compared to previous years, but still a large proportion, 52%, who did not meet this criterion, were omitted from computation of the official DA results above. High levels of low quality workers are consistent with what we have seen in DA used for crowd-sourced Machine Translation (Graham et al., 2016) and Video Captioning evaluations (Graham et al., 2017).

Results in Tables 13 and 14 are laid out as six separate tables one for each experiment run. The rank column indicates groups of systems where all systems have significantly higher scores than all systems in the next group below. Note that these groupings obscure some significant differences between systems within the same group. But because groups cannot be further subdivided in the sense above, systems within each group are of the same rank. Column 'Ave.' gives the average raw scores, 'Ave. z' the corresponding standard scores, *n* is the number distinct test sentences, and *N* the number of evaluators.

As can be seen from the tables, we included the 2019 submissions from two teams who submitted new systems in 2020: **BME-UW**'s and **IMS**'s English_ewt, Russian_syntagrus and Spanish_ancora outputs, in order to have comparable results. Results from the 2019 human evaluations are otherwise not comparable to the 2020 results, because a different set of systems was evaluated in each case. Absolute

[9]However, Tilburg and BME-UW show unexpected drops on some test sets that remain to be explained.

[10]`www.mturk.com`

Rank	Ave.	Ave. z	n	N	System
		English (ewt)			
1	92.6	0.540	1,698	1,931	ADAPT20BT1
	92.7	0.534	1,693	1,919	IMS20AT1
	92.3	0.520	1,683	1,912	IMS20BT1
	91.5	0.504	1,706	1,943	IMS19T1
	90.7	0.476	1,685	1,914	ADAPT20AT1
6	87.0	0.332	1,679	1,915	CONCORDIA20AT1
7	85.1	0.272	1,667	1,927	IMS20BT2
	84.7	0.259	1,701	1,942	IMS20AT2
	84.7	0.245	1,675	1,897	CONCORDIA20AT2
10	82.7	0.201	1,692	1,920	IMS19T2
11	79.3	0.086	1,679	1,925	BME20AT1
	77.4	0.024	1,690	1,933	BME19T1
13	75.6	−0.079	1,657	1,892	NILC20AT2

Rank	Ave.	Ave. z	n	N	System
		English (Wiki)			
1	94.7	0.638	699	1,043	ADAPT20BT1
2	93.7	0.535	719	1,072	IMS20BT1
	92.3	0.475	708	1,052	IMS20AT1
	91.6	0.444	715	1,061	IMS19T1
	91.6	0.441	718	1,115	ADAPT20AT1
6	88.7	0.275	707	1,038	CONCORDIA20AT1
7	87.3	0.157	700	1,016	IMS20BT2
8	85.6	0.057	755	1,078	IMS20AT2
	85.5	0.025	698	1,023	IMS19T2
	84.7	−0.029	715	1,036	CONCORDIA20AT2
	83.4	−0.033	698	1,033	TILBURG19T1
	81.8	−0.050	724	1,055	BME20AT1
	82.4	−0.074	721	1,056	BME19T1
	81.5	−0.118	689	1,021	RALI19T1
15	76.0	−0.463	720	1,044	RALI19T2
	76.6	−0.491	721	1,088	NILC20AT2

Rank	Ave.	Ave. z	n	N	System
		Russian (syntagrus)			
1	90.3	0.375	4,403	5,269	IMS20AT1
2	89.4	0.319	4,377	5,260	IMS20BT1
3	88.9	0.285	4,429	5,332	IMS19T1
4	81.2	−0.166	4,461	5,392	BME20AT1
	81.3	−0.177	4,466	5,371	BME19T1

Rank	Ave.	Ave. z	n	N	System
		Russian (wiki)			
1	89.1	0.490	722	963	IMS20AT1
2	88.1	0.396	724	947	IMS19T1
	87.2	0.382	728	972	IMS20BT1
4	78.2	−0.079	738	963	BME20AT1
5	73.7	−0.256	703	929	TILBURG19T1
6	68.2	−0.493	722	968	BME19T1

Rank	Ave.	Ave. z	n	N	System
		Spanish (ancora)			
1	89.8	0.518	1,233	1,491	IMS20AT1
	89.5	0.498	1,251	1,479	IMS20BT1
3	85.9	0.383	1,252	1,504	IMS19T1
4	77.9	0.037	1,184	1,421	IMS20AT2
	77.1	0.017	1,225	1,467	IMS20BT2
	76.8	−0.029	1,199	1,436	IMS19T2
7	70.6	−0.271	1,223	1,490	BME19T1
	70.2	−0.276	1,230	1,489	BME20AT1

Rank	Ave.	Ave. z	n	N	System
		Spanish (Wiki)			
1	87.6	0.557	879	1,167	IMS20BT1
	86.3	0.524	909	1,192	IMS20AT1
3	85.2	0.465	897	1,162	IMS19T1
4	76.9	0.123	847	1,088	IMS20BT2
	75.9	0.092	910	1,197	IMS20AT2
	75.4	0.063	880	1,124	IMS19T2
7	71.0	−0.119	894	1,173	TILBURG19T1
	69.8	−0.170	877	1,139	BME20AT1
9	55.5	−0.726	908	1,181	BME19T1

Table 13: Human evaluation results for **Meaning Similarity**. Ave. = average score received by systems; Ave. z = corresponding average standardized score; systems ranked according to Ave. z score; horizontal lines indicate groups, such that systems in a group all significantly outperform all systems in lower ranked groups; n = total number of distinct test sentences assessed; N = total number of human judgments.

scores (*Ave.*) are particularly affected by differences even from different sets of evaluators and output samples. Pairwise rankings for the same systems however, can be expected to be more robust.

The 2020 evaluations are indeed consistent with last year's in terms rankings according to z-scores: when a system was in a higher cluster than another in 2019, it is still the case in 2020. There are two exceptions, **IMS19T2** and **BME19T1** were together in the same cluster on Meaning Similarity and Readability for English_ewt, but this year appear in consecutive clusters. One explanation for this is that we collected considerably more judgements this year, and when there are more judgements, it is likely that more statistically significant differences are found, which seems to be the case here. Most of the standard scores are lower in 2020 than they were in 2019, and this is likely due to the fact that the best scoring systems score higher (e.g. 4 systems at the level or above the best 2019 system on English_ewt) which tends to push down the lower systems in terms of z score.

Looking at the 2020 results only, for both Meaning Similarity (Table 13) and Readability (Table 14), SR'20 systems are generally ranked higher than SR'19 systems, T1 systems are generally ranked higher than T2 systems, and where a system has both 'a' (restricted subtrack) and 'b' (open subtrack) variants, the 'b' system is ranked higher in most (though not all) cases. This is all as expected.

In terms of Meaning Similarity, the best score is higher than last year on all three comparable datasets: the best system obtains an average z score of 0.54 on English_ewt (0.507 in 2019), 0.375 on Russian_syntagrus (0.238), and 0.518 on Spanish_ancora (0.378). For Readability, the best z scores are 0.426, 0.546 and 0.446 respectively, compared to 0.507, 0.238 and 0.519 in 2019, that is, only for

Rank	Ave.	Ave. z	n	N	System
		English (ewt)			
1	75.7	0.426	797	913	ADAPT20BT1
–	75.7	0.417	669	1,402	HUMAN
	73.9	0.374	807	917	IMS20AT1
	73.9	0.370	810	927	IMS20BT1
	73.4	0.346	811	926	IMS19T1
	71.8	0.321	806	908	CONCORDIA20AT2
	72.5	0.320	830	953	ADAPT20AT1
	70.2	0.270	860	969	CONCORDIA20AT1
	68.6	0.185	823	947	NILC20AT2
	67.3	0.159	807	936	IMS20BT2
	65.8	0.109	753	866	IMS20AT2
11	63.6	0.027	808	923	IMS19T2
12	58.2	−0.152	839	946	BME20AT1
	56.7	−0.208	822	935	BME19T1

Rank	Ave.	Ave. z	n	N	System
		English (Wiki)			
–	87.4	0.592	955	2,605	HUMAN
1	86.3	0.551	910	1,274	ADAPT20BT1
2	83.3	0.444	938	1,302	IMS20BT1
	79.6	0.401	942	1,290	CONCORDIA20AT1
	82.1	0.383	949	1,314	IMS20AT1
	81.5	0.373	948	1,346	ADAPT20AT1
	80.6	0.370	952	1,283	CONCORDIA20AT2
	81.3	0.361	937	1,321	IMS19T1
8	75.4	0.213	930	1,273	NILC20AT2
9	70.2	0.055	932	1,256	IMS20BT2
	69.0	−0.030	963	1,284	IMS20AT2
11	67.3	−0.095	932	1,233	IMS19T2
	67.8	−0.128	932	1,306	TILBURG19T1
13	64.4	−0.181	897	1,239	BME19T1
14	60.8	−0.299	933	1,297	BME20AT1
	62.3	−0.303	912	1,242	RALI19T1
16	56.1	−0.562	940	1,329	RALI19T2

Rank	Ave.	Ave. z	n	N	System
		Russian (syntagrus)			
–	93.5	0.635	499	689	HUMAN
1	90.8	0.546	943	1,068	IMS20AT1
2	89.1	0.489	972	1,106	IMS20BT1
3	87.3	0.424	949	1,085	IMS19T1
4	69.7	−0.166	966	1,106	BME20AT1
	67.3	−0.230	943	1,078	BME19T1

Rank	Ave.	Ave. z	n	N	System
		Russian (Wiki)			
–	92.6	0.924	414	658	HUMAN
1	85.5	0.720	695	897	IMS20AT1
2	83.1	0.643	677	868	IMS19T1
	83.1	0.635	705	916	IMS20BT1
4	63.2	0.050	703	900	BME20AT1
5	47.9	−0.415	710	911	TILBURG19T1
6	37.7	−0.781	679	883	BME19T1

Rank	Ave.	Ave. z	n	N	System
		Spanish (ancora)			
–	90.7	0.595	676	1,110	HUMAN
1	87.6	0.446	944	1,164	IMS20AT1
	86.7	0.433	929	1,144	IMS20BT1
	85.8	0.391	920	1,112	IMS19T1
4	80.2	0.173	923	1,127	IMS20BT2
	79.5	0.158	933	1,149	IMS20AT2
6	77.0	0.066	923	1,157	IMS19T2
7	67.1	−0.378	923	1,155	BME19T1
	66.4	−0.401	906	1,125	BME20AT1

Rank	Ave.	Ave. z	n	N	System
		Spanish (Wiki)			
–	87.7	0.371	524	798	HUMAN
1	86.5	0.289	643	733	IMS20AT1
	85.6	0.249	623	721	IMS20BT1
	84.9	0.237	620	715	IMS19T1
4	81.5	0.142	620	711	IMS20BT2
	79.3	0.046	619	713	IMS20AT2
	79.0	0.044	637	725	IMS19T2
	77.2	0.015	574	663	BME20AT1
	74.8	−0.053	614	699	TILBURG19T1
9	62.2	−0.628	592	679	BME19T1

Table 14: Human evaluation results for **Readability**. Ave. = average score for system; Ave. z = corresponding average standardized score; systems ranked by Ave. z score; horizontal lines indicate groups, such that systems in a group all significantly outperform all systems in lower ranked groups; n = distinct test sentences assessed; N = total number of judgments; HUMAN = original reference texts.

the Russian dataset the absolute z score is higher. However, both in English and Spanish, the human references are also scored lower,

On the English_ewt dataset, for both criteria , **ADAPT** and **IMS** get all their T1 submissions in the first rank (including the 2019 one for **IMS**); for Readability, **Concordia**'s T1 and T2 submissions, **NILC**'s T2 and **IMS**'s T2 also make it to the first cluster, which contains 10 systems. It is the first time that some T2 submissions make it to the same cluster as the human-written references. In terms of Meaning Similarity, three of the four T2 top-ranking submissions are found at the seventh rank, in the third cluster (**IMS**'s and **Concordia**'s 2020 submissions); **NILC** ranks last in for this criterion, indicating that although the generated texts read well, they do not contain the expected information.

IMS's restricted track T1 submissions ranks in the first cluster for all four non-English datasets according to both criteria. Note that this is consistent with the results of the automatic evaluations, in which even though **IMS**'s open track systems gets overall better results, it is not the case on every individual dataset. On the Spanish Wikipedia dataset, **IMS** gets their three T1 submissions in the same cluster as the human-written texts (Readability), while also scoring high in terms of Meaning Similarity. Here again it is the first time that a system gets at a level where it is statistically not significantly ranked lower than a human reference in a non-English language.

On the English_wiki dataset, **ADAPT** ranks first for both criteria, and is the only one in the same clus-

	BLEU	NIST	DIST	BERT	Read.
English (ewt)	0.94^{**}	0.85^{**}	0.97^{**}	0.94^{**}	0.78^{**}
English (Wiki)	0.95^{**}	0.92^{**}	0.97^{**}	0.97^{**}	0.74^{**}
Russian (syntagrus)	1.00^{**}	0.98^{**}	1.00^{**}	0.97^{**}	1.00^{**}
Russian (Wiki)	0.99^{**}	0.88^{**}	0.98^{**}	0.99^{**}	0.99^{**}
Spanish (ancora)	0.87^{**}	0.72^{*}	0.98^{**}	0.97^{**}	0.95^{**}
Spanish (Wiki)	0.94^{**}	0.80^{**}	0.99^{**}	0.99^{**}	0.95^{**}

Table 15: Pearson correlation of BLEU, NIST, DIST, BERT and Readability scores with human assessment of Meaning Similarity Ave z. ** = significant at p< 0.01; * = significant at p< 0.05.

	BLEU	NIST	DIST	BERT	Mean. Sim.
English (ewt)	0.69^{**}	0.39	0.82^{**}	0.70^{**}	0.78^{**}
English (Wiki)	0.79^{**}	0.62^{**}	0.81^{**}	0.81^{**}	0.74^{**}
Russian (syntagrus)	1.00^{**}	0.99^{**}	1.00^{**}	0.96^{**}	1.00^{**}
Russian (Wiki)	1.00^{**}	0.91^{**}	0.97^{**}	0.99^{**}	0.99^{**}
Spanish (ancora)	0.67^{*}	0.47	0.98^{**}	0.87^{**}	0.95^{**}
Spanish (Wiki)	0.92^{**}	0.77^{**}	0.96^{**}	0.97^{**}	0.95^{**}

Table 16: Pearson correlation of BLEU, NIST, DIST, BERT and Meaning Similarity scores with human assessment of Readability Ave z. ** = significant at p< 0.01; * = significant at p< 0.05.

ter as the human references for Readability. The very high scores of **ADAPT** reflect the also very strong automatic evaluation (94 BLEU, see previous subsection). On this dataset, the gap between **ADAPT** and the other systems was a little bit surprising, and we realised that it used models trained on WikiText-103 (Merity et al., 2016), which seems to contain a small proportion of the sentences of the test set. This was of course not something done on purpose by the team, since the participants did not know that the new test sets would contain exclusively Wikipedia material. Note that **IMS**'s 2019 system remains extremely competitive on this dataset, outperforming all other submissions except **ADAPT**. The other 2019 systems (**Tilburg**, **RALI**, **BME-UW**) occupy the lower ranks as expected, with **NILC**'s T2 submission.

6.3 Comparisons between human and automatic evaluations

In this section, we compare the metrics results presented in Section 6.1 with human evaluation results presented in Section 6.2 first informally, then more systematically, in two ways. First in terms of Pearson correlation of metrics with Meaning Similarity z scores (Table 15) and Readability z scores (Table 16), both at the test set level; second by plotting all system scores for the T2_en_ewt test set in groups by system, once in decreasing order of Meaning Similarity scores (Figure 4), and once in decreasing order of Readability scores (Figure 5).

In terms of human and automatic metrics for individual systems, the **IMS** 2020 results are very high both in terms of automatic evaluations and human assessments for many of the languages offered, and represent a substantial improvement over their 2019 system, both through method improvement (higher results despite using the same data resources for training), and through using better data (open track results). **ADAPT** got very high automatic and human scores in the open subtrack for the English T1 test sets compared to other English T1 submissions, to the point of drawing level with the human en_ewt texts for Readability (Table 14, top left). **Concordia** obtained the highest Readability scores on the English T2 submissions, while matching the **IMS** Meaning Similarity scores; however, the corresponding metric scores were lower. Overall, **IMS**, **ADAPT**, **BME-TUW** and **Concordia** all achieved major improvements in their systems. The **NILC** results appear to show the limitations of using an off-the-shelf generic model.

There are indications that we do capture different aspects with the two quality criteria. For instance, **NILC** gets good Readability scores but low Meaning Similarity, which is typical of generative models like GPT-2, which are able to generate very good texts but without ensuring that they correspond to the input fed to the system. **Concordia**'s T2 submissions seems to have similar features, even though it scores consistently higher than **NILC**'s submission.

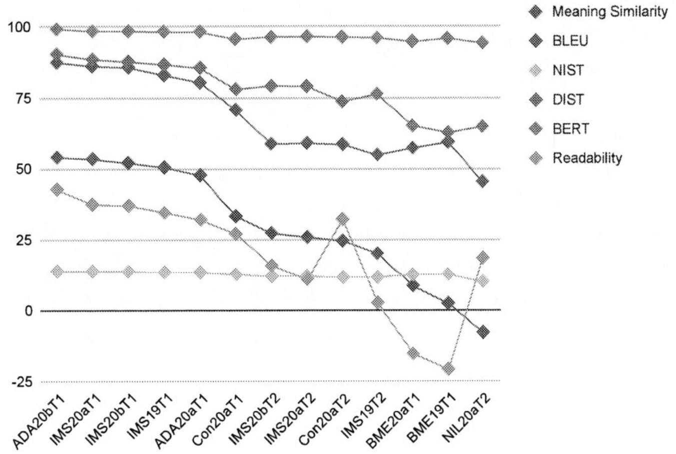

Figure 4: Visualisation of the scores of the 13 submissions on the English_ewt dataset according to the 6 metrics. On the X axis, the systems as ranked by Meaning Similarity Ave. z in Table 13.[12]

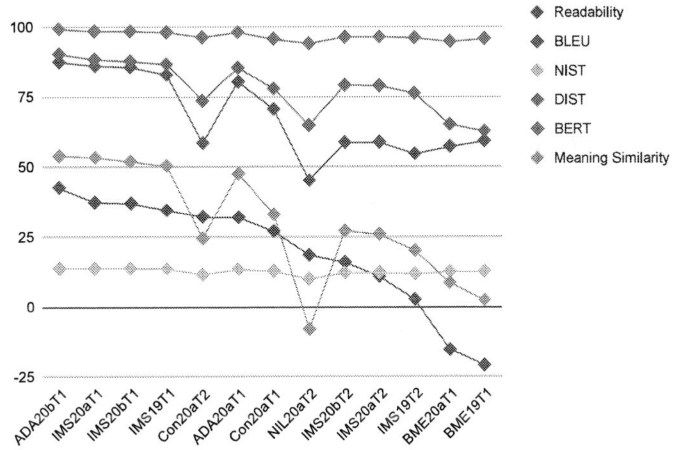

Figure 5: Visualisation of the scores of the 13 submissions on the English_ewt dataset according to the 6 metrics. On the X axis, the systems as ranked by Readability Ave. z in Table 14.[12]

Regarding correlations of metrics with Meaning Similarity, Table 15 shows these to be generally in the mid to high nineties, with isolated lower scores, e.g. for BLEU on Spanish_ancora. One notable exception is the lower correlation of Meaning Similarity with Readability on the English test sets. This may be due to English outputs being of higher quality generally than those for other languages, and evaluators finding it easier to judge Meaning Similarity separately when sentences are more readable.

Regarding correlations of metrics with Readability (Table 16), the quality criterion generally supposed to correlate better with metrics, there are more cases of lower correlation including all scores for both English test sets, as well as BLEU, NIST and BERT for Spanish_ancora and NIST for Spanish_wiki. For the Russian test sets, all correlations are exceptionally high.

For Readability, the reported correlations are noticeably lower than the ones reported in both 2018 and 2019. One possible explanation is that in the previous years, the differences between the systems were very clear, but now we have many more good systems, so it is more difficult for the automatic metrics

[12]Lines have been added to the plot to show up clearly which scores are for the same evaluation method, even in black and white version.

to capture the differences between them. This year, in contrast to SR'19, the DIST metric has the most consistently high correlation scores with the human evaluation methods.

Figure 4 plots results for all systems on English_ewt, with score points for each evaluation method connected by a line to indicate that they are for the same method, systems ordered across the x dimension in order of decreasing Meaning Similarity. From the plot we can see clearly that, as Meaning Similarity goes down, generally so do the metrics, and also Readability except for scores for **Concordia20aT2** and **NILC20aT2** which buck the trend.

Figure 5 shows a similar plot, this time ordered by decreasing Readability. This shows very clearly that all metrics and Meaning Similarity scores dip at the same two points, **Concordia20aT2** and **NILC20aT2**, although this is less evident for BERT and NIST scores (in the latter case because NIST has a very different range from the other evaluation methods and because it is not bounded at the top end cannot simply be mapped to a 0–1 range). So here too, it is clear that for those two systems, Readability is lower than would be expected on the basis of all other evaluation methods including human assessment of Meaning Similarity.

7 Concluding Remarks

The 2020 edition of the SR Shared Task (SR'20) saw 5 teams submitting new systems and 4 teams submitting outputs for the new test sets using their 2019 systems. Datasets, evaluation scripts, system outputs and more information about the shared task can be found on the GenChal repository.[13]

Among the notable trends we can observe in evaluations this year are the following: (i) the best Shallow Track English systems appear to have closed the gap to human-written texts in terms of all evaluation measures; (ii) for the first time we have seen outputs for a non-English language (Spanish) approach the quality of human-written reference texts; and (iii) allowing additional resources to be used in system building can make a very big difference to performance. Further progress has also been made in SR'20 for deep track systems: the best Deep Track system performed equally well or better than most Shallow Track systems for both Readability and Meaning similarity.

Overall, the SR'20 results provide further evidence that generation from structured meaning representations can be done with impressive success by current neural methods. Our aim for next year's edition of the shared task is to add linked tasks corresponding to an earlier stage in the generation process, asking for submissions which use the intermediate UD representations as well as submissions that by-pass them in order to compare which gives better results overall.

Acknowledgements

SR'20 is endorsed by SIGGEN. The work on the organisation, realisation, and evaluation of this shared task was supported by (1) the European Commission in the context of its H2020 Program under the grant numbers 870930-RIA, 779962-RIA, 825079-RIA, 786731-RIA at Universitat Pompeu Fabra; (2) the Applied Data Analytics Research & Enterprise Group, University of Brighton, UK, (3) Science Foundation Ireland (sfi.ie) under the SFI Research Centres Programme co-funded under the European Regional Development Fund, grant number 13/RC/2106 (ADAPT Centre for Digital Content Technology, www.adaptcentre.ie) at Trinity College Dublin; and (4) the Coordination for the Improvement of Higher Education Personnel in Brazil (CAPES) under the grant 88887.508597/2020-00.

References

Rami Al-Rfou, Bryan Perozzi, and Steven Skiena. 2013. Polyglot: Distributed word representations for multilingual NLP. In *Proceedings of the Seventeenth Conference on Computational Natural Language Learning*, pages 183–192, Sofia, Bulgaria, August. Association for Computational Linguistics.

G. Awad, A. Butt, K. Curtis, Y. Lee, J. Fiscus, A. Godil, A. Delgado, J. Zhang, E. Godard, L. Diduch, A. F. Smeaton, Y. Graham, and W. Kraaij. 2019. Trecvid 2019: An evaluation campaign to benchmark video activity

[13]https://sites.google.com/site/genchalrepository/surface-realisation/sr-20-multilingual

detection, video captioning and matching, and video search & retrieval. In *Proceedings of TRECVID*, volume 2019.

Loïc Barrault, Ondřej Bojar, Marta R. Costa-jussà, Christian Federmann, Mark Fishel, Yvette Graham, Barry Haddow, Matthias Huck, Philipp Koehn, Shervin Malmasi, Christof Monz, Mathias Müller, Santanu Pal, Matt Post, and Marcos Zampieri. 2019. Findings of the 2019 conference on machine translation (wmt19). In *Proceedings of the Fourth Conference on Machine Translation (Volume 2: Shared Task Papers, Day 1)*, pages 1–61, Florence, Italy, August. Association for Computational Linguistics.

Loïc Barrault, Ondřej Bojar, Fethi Bougares, Rajen Chatterjee, Marta R. Costa-jussà, Christian Federmann, Mark Fishel, Alexander Fraser, Yvette Graham, Paco Guzman, Barry Haddow, Matthias Huck, Antonio Jimeno Yepes, Philipp Koehn, André Martins, Makoto Morishita, Christof Monz, Masaaki Nagata, Toshiaki Nakazawa, and Matteo Negri, editors. 2020. *Proceedings of the Fifth Conference on Machine Translation*. Association for Computational Linguistics, Online, November.

Anya Belz and Eric Kow. 2011. Discrete vs. continuous rating scales for language evaluation in NLP. In *Proceedings of the 49th Annual Meeting of the Association for Computational Linguistics (ACL-HLT'11)*.

Anya Belz, Michael White, Dominic Espinosa, Eric Kow, Deirdre Hogan, and Amanda Stent. 2011. The first surface realisation shared task: Overview and evaluation results. In *Proceedings of the 13th European Workshop on Natural Language Generation*, ENLG '11, pages 217–226, Stroudsburg, PA, USA. Association for Computational Linguistics.

Wanxiang Che, Jiang Guo, Yuxuan Wang, Bo Zheng, Huaipeng Zhao, Yang Liu, Dechuan Teng, and Ting Liu. 2017. The hit-scir system for end-to-end parsing of universal dependencies. In *Proceedings of the CoNLL 2017 Shared Task: Multilingual Parsing from Raw Text to Universal Dependencies*, pages 52–62.

Jacob Devlin, Ming-Wei Chang, Kenton Lee, and Kristina Toutanova. 2018. Bert: Pre-training of deep bidirectional transformers for language understanding. *arXiv preprint arXiv:1810.04805*.

Ondřej Dušek, David M Howcroft, and Verena Rieser. 2019. Semantic noise matters for neural natural language generation. *arXiv preprint arXiv:1911.03905*.

Thiago Castro Ferreira and Emiel Krahmer. 2019. Surface Realization Shared Task 2019 (SR'19): The Tilburg University Approach. In *Proceedings of the 2nd Workshop on Multilingual Surface Realisation*, Hong Kong, China.

Thiago Castro Ferreira, Sander Wubben, and Emiel Krahmer. 2018. Surface realization shared task 2018 (sr18): The tilburg university approach. In *Proceedings of the First Workshop on Multilingual Surface Realisation*, pages 35–38.

Yvette Graham, Timothy Baldwin, Alistair Moffat, and Justin Zobel. 2016. Can machine translation systems be evaluated by the crowd alone. *Natural Language Engineering*, FirstView:1–28, 1.

Yvette Graham, George Awad, and Alan Smeaton. 2017. Evaluation of Automatic Video Captioning Using Direct Assessment. *ArXiv e-prints*, October.

Yvette Graham, George Awad, and Alan Smeaton. 2018. Evaluation of automatic video captioning using direct assessment. *PLOS ONE*, 13(9):1–20, 09.

Yvette Graham, Barry Haddow, and Philipp Koehn. 2019. Translationese in machine translation evaluation. *CoRR*, abs/1906.09833.

Karl Moritz Hermann, Tomas Kocisky, Edward Grefenstette, Lasse Espeholt, Will Kay, Mustafa Suleyman, and Phil Blunsom. 2015. Teaching machines to read and comprehend. In *Advances in neural information processing systems*, pages 1693–1701.

Xinyu Hua and Lu Wang. 2019. Sentence-level content planning and style specification for neural text generation.

Adám Kovács, Evelin Ács, Judit Ács, András Kornai, and Gábor Recski. 2019. BME-UW at SR'19: Surface Realization with Interpreted Regular Tree Grammars. In *Proceedings of the 2nd Workshop on Multilingual Surface Realisation*, Hong Kong, China.

Guy Lapalme. 2019. Realizing Universal Dependencies Structures Using a Symbolic Approach. In *Proceedings of the 2nd Workshop on Multilingual Surface Realisation*, Hong Kong, China.

Mike Lewis, Yinhan Liu, Naman Goyal, Marjan Ghazvininejad, Abdelrahman Mohamed, Omer Levy, Veselin Stoyanov, and Luke Zettlemoyer. 2020. BART: Denoising sequence-to-sequence pre-training for natural language generation, translation, and comprehension. In *Proceedings of the 58th Annual Meeting of the Association for Computational Linguistics*, pages 7871–7880, Online, July. Association for Computational Linguistics.

KyungTae Lim, Cheoneum Park, Changki Lee, and Thierry Poibeau. 2018. Sex bist: A multi-source trainable parser with deep contextualized lexical representations. In *Proceedings of the CoNLL 2018 Shared Task: Multilingual Parsing from Raw Text to Universal Dependencies*, pages 143–152.

Qingsong Ma, Yvette Graham, Timothy Baldwin, and Qun Liu. 2017. Further investigation into reference bias in monolingual evaluation of machine translation. In *Proceedings of the 2017 Conference on Empirical Methods in Natural Language Processing*, pages 2466–2475, Copenhagen, Denmark, September. Association for Computational Linguistics.

Stephen Merity, Caiming Xiong, James Bradbury, and Richard Socher. 2016. Pointer sentinel mixture models. *arXiv preprint arXiv:1609.07843*.

Simon Mille, Bernd Bohnet, Leo Wanner, and Anja Belz. 2017. Shared task proposal: Multilingual surface realization using universal dependency trees. In *Proceedings of the 10th International Conference on Natural Language Generation*, pages 120–123.

Simon Mille, Anya Belz, Bernd Bohnet, Yvette Graham, Emily Pitler, and Leo Wanner. 2018. The First Multilingual Surface Realisation Shared Task (SR'18): Overview and Evaluation Results. In *Proceedings of the 1st Workshop on Multilingual Surface Realisation (MSR), 56th Annual Meeting of the Association for Computational Linguistics (ACL)*, pages 1–12, Melbourne, Australia.

Simon Mille, Anya Belz, Bernd Bohnet, Yvette Graham, and Leo Wanner. 2019. The second multilingual surface realisation shared task (sr'19): Overview and evaluation results. In *Proceedings of the 2nd Workshop on Multilingual Surface Realisation (MSR 2019)*, pages 1–17.

Paul Molins and Guy Lapalme. 2015. Jsrealb: A bilingual text realizer for web programming. In *Proceedings of the 15th European Workshop on Natural Language Generation (ENLG)*, pages 109–111.

K. Papineni, S. Roukos, T. Ward, and W. j. Zhu. 2002. BLEU: A method for automatic evaluation of machine translation. In *Proc. 40th Annual Meeting on Association for Computational Linguistics*, pages 311–318, Philadelphia, Pennsylvania, July 7–12,.

Matthew E Peters, Mark Neumann, Mohit Iyyer, Matt Gardner, Christopher Clark, Kenton Lee, and Luke Zettlemoyer. 2018. Deep contextualized word representations. *arXiv preprint arXiv:1802.05365*.

Peng Qi, Timothy Dozat, Yuhao Zhang, and Christopher D Manning. 2019. Universal dependency parsing from scratch. *arXiv preprint arXiv:1901.10457*.

Peng Qi, Yuhao Zhang, Yuhui Zhang, Jason Bolton, and Christopher D. Manning. 2020. Stanza: A Python natural language processing toolkit for many human languages. In *Proceedings of the 58th Annual Meeting of the Association for Computational Linguistics: System Demonstrations*.

Alec Radford, Jeff Wu, Rewon Child, David Luan, Dario Amodei, and Ilya Sutskever. 2019. Language models are unsupervised multitask learners. *OpenAI Blog*, 1(8).

Aaron Smith, Bernd Bohnet, Miryam de Lhoneux, Joakim Nivre, Yan Shao, and Sara Stymne. 2018. 82 treebanks, 34 models: Universal dependency parsing with cross-treebank models. In *Proceedings of the CoNLL 2018 Shared Task: Multilingual Parsing from Raw Text to Universal Dependencies*. Asso. for Comp. Linguistics.

Xiang Yu, Agnieszka Falenska, Marina Haid, Ngoc Thang Vu, and Jonas Kuhn. 2019. IMSurReal: IMS at the Surface Realization Shared Task 2019. In *Proceedings of the 2nd Workshop on Multilingual Surface Realisation*, Hong Kong, China.

Xiang Yu, Simon Tannert, Ngoc Thang Vu, and Jonas Kuhn. 2020. Fast and accurate non-projective dependency tree linearization. In *Proceedings of the 58th Annual Meeting of the Association for Computational Linguistics*, pages 1451–1462, Online, July. Association for Computational Linguistics.

Fangzhou Zhai, Vera Demberg, Pavel Shkadzko, Wei Shi, and Asad Sayeed. 2019. A hybrid model for globally coherent story generation. In *Proceedings of the Second Workshop on Storytelling*, pages 34–45.

Tianyi Zhang, Varsha Kishore, Felix Wu, Kilian Q. Weinberger, and Yoav Artzi. 2020. Bertscore: Evaluating text generation with bert.

Liang Zhao, Jingjing Xu, Junyang Lin, Yichang Zhang, Hongxia Yang, and Xu Sun. 2020. Graph-based multi-hop reasoning for long text generation. *arXiv preprint arXiv:2009.13282*.

BME-TUW at SR'20: Lexical grammar induction for surface realization

Gábor Recski[1], Ádám Kovács[1,2], Kinga Gémes[1,2], Judit Ács[2], András Kornai[3]

[1]TU Wien
firstname.lastname@tuwien.ac.at

[2]Dept. of Automation and Applied Informatics, Budapest U of Technology
lastname.firstname@aut.bme.hu

[3]SZTAKI Institute of Computer Science
andras@kornai.com

Abstract

We present a system for mapping Universal Dependency structures to raw text which learns to restore word order by training an Interpreted Regular Tree Grammar (IRTG) that establishes a mapping between string and graph operations. The reinflection step is handled by a standard sequence-to-sequence architecture with a biLSTM encoder and an LSTM decoder with attention. We modify our 2019 system (Kovács et al., 2019) with a new grammar induction mechanism that allows IRTG rules to operate on lemmata in addition to part-of-speech tags and ensures that each word and its dependents are reordered using the most specific set of learned patterns. We also introduce a hierarchical approach to word order restoration that independently determines the word order of each clause in a sentence before arranging them with respect to the main clause, thereby improving overall readability and also making the IRTG parsing task tractable. We participated in the 2020 Surface Realization Shared task, subtrack T1a (shallow, closed). Human evaluation shows we achieve significant improvements on two of the three out-of-domain datasets compared to the 2019 system we modified. Both components of our system are available on GitHub under an MIT license.

1 Introduction

This paper describes our participation in the T1a subtask of the 2020 Surface Realization Shared Task (Mille et al., 2020), which requires systems to map Universal Dependency graphs of lemmata to raw sentences by reconstructing word forms and word order. We extend the word order restoration component of Kovács et al. (2019) by making it sensitive to lemmata in addition to parts-of-speech and by performing the word order restoration step separately for each clause of a sentence. The paper is structured as follows: Section 2 briefly describes the data and the task as well as the architecture that we modify. Section 3 presents our new method for rule generation for creating lexical grammars, Section 4 describes the hierarchical approach for breaking up the word order restoration task into clause-level subtasks. Section 6 presents a summary of both automatic and human evaluations, Section 7 discusses potential future work. The IRTG-based system for word order restoration can be downloaded from https://github.com/adaamko/surface_realization, the inflection system was trained using the framework under https://github.com/juditacs/deep-morphology. Both components are available for download under an MIT license.

Proceedings of the Third Workshop on Multilingual Surface Realisation (MSR'20), pages 21–29
Barcelona, Spain (Online), December 12, 2020.

2 Background

2.1 SRST

The 2020 Surface Realization Shared Task (Mille et al., 2020) involves mapping Universal Dependency representations to raw text. The input data in the shallow track consists of UD-annotated sentences for 11 languages, without word order information and without inflected word forms, i.e. they are typed dependency graphs of lemmata of a sentence. The task is to reproduce the original sentences, which involves reconstructing word order and inflected word forms. The primary method of evaluation is human judgments of readability and fidelity of output sentences to the original, but automatic metrics are also used to measure the similarity between predicted and gold standard sentences.

The system presented in this paper, a substantial extension of the solution of Kovács et al. (2019), offers a fully rule-based, explainable, and language-independent solution for the word order restoration component of the shallow surface realization task and uses an independent ML system for reconstructing word forms. In last year's evaluation, the top rule-based systems were consistently outperformed by the best-performing IMS (Yu et al., 2019) and CMU (Du and Black, 2019) systems (see Mille et al. (2019) for evaluation details). Both of these solutions rely on deep learning models for the word order restoration component of the task. Still, an important similarity between their approaches and ours is that they also take the *divide-and-conquer* approach of determining word order separately for each head and all its dependents. In future work this will allow detailed comparison between the atomic decisions of our system and the state-of-the-art (see Section 7 for some proposals).

2.2 IRTGs for surface realization

The system presented in this paper is based on the architecture presented in Kovács et al. (2019), which involves the induction of an Interpreted Regular Tree Grammar (Koller, 2015) whose rules establish a mapping between operations of i) a string algebra that concatenates words and phrases of a sentence and ii) an algebra over graphs that builds UD structures by merging nodes and subgraphs. We briefly outline the architecture of this system and refer the reader to the original paper for details.

An IRTG rule is a (possibly weighted) rewrite rule of a Regular Tree Grammar that is mapped to an arbitrary number of named *interpretations*, each of which are operations of an algebra with the same arity as the RTG rule. Thereby any particular derivation of an IRTG grammar deterministically maps to a sequence of operations in each of the interpretation algebras. Parsing an object of one algebra involves finding the IRTG derivation(s) of the highest likelihood that would generate this object, while *decoding* is the subsequent construction of an object in another algebra using this sequence. The word reordering task is then equivalent to parsing graphs and decoding strings using an IRTG with two interpretations.

UD graphs have the property that the indegree of each node is exactly 1, i.e. each word is the dependent of exactly one other word in the sentence (this is achieved by introducing the dummy `ROOT` element that governs the root word in the sentence). This allows us to straightforwardly model the construction of UD graphs as a sequence of operations that each connect a word to all its dependents. The word order restoration task can then be modeled as the correspondence between a sequence of operations in a graph algebra building such an UD subgraph and the string operations concatenating the words of this subgraph in a particular order. Since the system operates on POS-tags, not word forms, an example would be the steps for building the UD subgraph $\texttt{VERB} \xrightarrow{\text{nsubj}} \texttt{NOUN}$, which in a model for English would be expected to correspond to the concatenation operations yielding the string `NOUN VERB`. An IRTG rule encoding this correspondence can be seen in Figure 1: an RTG rule followed by its two interpretations, i.e. operations in a string algebra and an s-graph algebra as they are to be applied to the string and s-graph objects corresponding to each of the nonterminals on the right hand side of the RTG rule. For lack of space we do not describe the operation of the s-graph algebra in detail, but see the original system description (Kovács et al., 2019) for an overview and Koller and Kuhlmann (2011) or Courcelle and Engelfriet (2012) for more formal explanations. Grammars are built by inducing IRTG rules from sentences in the training data, and rule weights correspond to the observed frequencies of individual patterns. Parsing and decoding are performed using the open-source `alto` library[1] (Gontrum et al., 2017).

```
VERB -> _nsubj(VERB, NOUN)
[string] *(?2, ?1)
[ud] f_dep1(merge(merge(?1, "(r<root> :nsubj d1<dep1>)"), r_dep1(?2)))
```

Figure 1: Example of an IRTG rule

Our main contribution is a number of substantial modifications of the grammar induction process of the above system, which we shall present in detail in Sections 3 and 4. First, the system presented above does not have access to lemmata and operates on graphs of POS-tags only, therefore it cannot learn about constructions that are typical of a lexical item but not its grammatical class. Second, its handling of unseen patterns is rudimentary: if a particular pattern of head POS and set of dependent POS tags has not been observed in the training data, the system will employ binary branching rules, i.e. the derivation will attach dependents to the head one-by-one. In the next sections we develop an architecture for inducing a lexical grammar that relies on lemma-level observations in the training data to cover each input UD graph with the most specific rules possible.

3 Lexical rule induction

3.1 Motivation

This section will describe our extension of the grammar induction system of Kovács et al. (2019) to include rules operating on lemmata in addition to those that refer to part-of-speech tags only. In modeling the construction of UD structures we preserve the fundamental assumption that the directed graphs of words are built as a series of operations which connect some set of dependents to their common head. In other words, the first argument of each rule in our grammar corresponds to a node from which outgoing dependency edges are to be added pointing to the nodes corresponding to the remaining arguments. The rule presented in Figure 1, which establishes an `nsubj` relation between a pair of words with the POS-tags `VERB` and `NOUN`, is recursive; the nonterminal `VERB` appearing on both sides of the RTG rule ensures that an arbitrary number of rules can be applied that connect dependents to the same head. Thus, all possible derivations of a given UD graph will have in common that for each word they eventually create the subgraph consisting of that word and all its dependents, but the number of possible RTG derivations that can generate a subgraph with $N+1$ nodes is 2^N, while the number of IRTG derivations are doubly exponential since a rule with arity k can have $k!$ different string interpretations. The complexity of the parsing problem for a given sentence was reduced in the original system by including in the grammar only those patterns that we have observed in the training data (i.e. a rule such as that in Figure 1 will be added to our grammar if and only if the subgraph `VERB` $\xrightarrow{nsubj}$ `NOUN` was observed in the training data without additional edges outgoing from the verb head), a constraint that would most likely cause data sparsity issues if we were to extend the process from POS-tags to word forms without fundamental modifications.

Our new approach to grammar induction differs from that of Kovács et al. (2019) in multiple ways. First, by including rules that can take lemmas instead of POS-tags as some or all of its arguments, the number of patterns matching a subgraph of $N+1$ nodes increases from 2^N to 3^N and the number of IRTG rules that under our original approach would be included in a grammar pruned for a sentence of average size would no longer be tractable. On the other hand, we expect that derivations including rules that operate directly on word forms should generally take precedence as more specific accounts of the same phenomenon. This expectation is in part based on the observation in Kovács et al. (2019) that choosing shorter derivations, i.e. those using fewer rules with higher arity to generate the same graph actually yields better results on the word order restoration task by virtue of being more specific. An example for this was the sentence *I really enjoyed reading it* in the `en_ewt-ud-dev` dataset. For the corresponding

[1] `https://github.com/coli-saar/alto`

PRON	$\xleftarrow{nsubj}$	VERB		PRON	$\xleftarrow{nsubj}$	VERB	$\xrightarrow{obj}$	PRON
PRON	$\xleftarrow{nsubj}$	enjoy		PRON	$\xleftarrow{nsubj}$	VERB	$\xrightarrow{obj}$	it
He	$\xleftarrow{nsubj}$	VERB		PRON	$\xleftarrow{nsubj}$	enjoy	$\xrightarrow{obj}$	PRON
He	$\xleftarrow{nsubj}$	enjoy		He	$\xleftarrow{nsubj}$	VERB	$\xrightarrow{obj}$	PRON
VERB	$\xrightarrow{obj}$	it		PRON	$\xleftarrow{nsubj}$	enjoy	$\xrightarrow{obj}$	it
VERB	$\xrightarrow{obj}$	PRON		He	$\xleftarrow{nsubj}$	VERB	$\xrightarrow{obj}$	it
enjoy	$\xrightarrow{obj}$	PRON		He	$\xleftarrow{nsubj}$	enjoy	$\xrightarrow{obj}$	PRON
enjoy	$\xrightarrow{obj}$	it		He	$\xleftarrow{nsubj}$	enjoy	$\xrightarrow{obj}$	it

Figure 2: Subgraphs generated for the sentence *He enjoyed it*

UD graph the most likely (and correct) derivation included a rule connecting four dependents of the root verb simultaneously and constructing the sequence of POS-tags `PRP RB VBD VBG`, corresponding to the word order *I really enjoyed reading*. The next-best parse would have constructed the sentece *I enjoyed really reading it* using a separate rule to attach the edge `VBD` $\xrightarrow{advmod}$ `RB` that yields the word order *enjoy really*. When extending the grammar induction process to lemmata, we expect that such a rule could be overridden by a more specific one for adding *enjoy* $\xrightarrow{advmod}$ *really* that yields the correct word order based on what we observed in the training data. Indeed, not only does our final system yield the correct word order for this sentence, it does so using a rule that explicitly maps the subgraph *I* $\xleftarrow{nsubj}$ *enjoy* $\xrightarrow{advmod}$ *really* to the string *I really enjoy*, a construction observed five times in the training data.

3.2 Method

Our method for word order restoration involves a training step for counting all word- and POS-level subgraphs in the training data along with the corresponding word orders, a grammar construction step that for each input UD structure creates an IRTG with the most frequent rules corresponding to each of its subgraphs, and the parsing and decoding of the UD graphs using the constructed IRTG and the `alto` library. Our surface realization system performs the last two steps separately for each clause of each sentence, for details see Section 4. We now describe the three core steps in detail.

The training step involves traversing the UD graphs of all sentences in the training dataset for a given language. For each word in the graph with at least one dependent we take the subgraph containing this word and all its dependents, and for each of these we enumerate all its subgraphs that contain the head and at least one additional node. Finally for each of these subgraphs we generate all possible combinations such that some of the nodes are represented by their part-of-speech tags and the others by their lemma. For a head word with N dependents this means enumerating $2 \cdot (3^N - 1)$ subgraphs (since the head of the structure must be present in the subgraph and it must have at least one edge). Figure 2 shows an example of subgraphs generated for the simple 3-node graph *enjoy*/`VERB` $\xrightarrow{obj}$ *it*/`PRON`. The total number of unique subgraphs observed in the training data for each language is listed in Table 1. For each subgraph we then consider the relative order of the nodes in the surface form of the sentence and increment a counter corresponding to the particular ordering on the particular subgraph. Finally, for each pattern we sort all observed orderings by frequency.

At the time of performing word order restoration on an UD graph we enumerate all patterns in the input graph and query the model for the most frequent word order, allowing us to create an IRTG rule whose two interpretations correspond to the graph operations building the particular pattern and the string operations concatenating the corresponding words in the order that is most typical of that pattern based on the training data. The test dataset also specifies the relative order of some elements with respect to their heads using the `lin` feature. When such information is present, we use it to skip contradictory orderings regardless of their observed frequency. Patterns containing more than 4 dependents in addition to the head are discarded to reduce parsing complexity. We expect this to have negligible effect on parsing quality because patterns this large are likely the result of superposing subpatterns already inferable from the data. It is possible, for our method to yield a grammar that does not cover the input UD graph, this

Lang	N_{patt}	D_{max}	$\|V\|$	D_{words}	N_{tok}
ar	8.6M	4.8	14K	36.9	224K
en	29.8M	5.0	25K	17.6	352K
es	50.2M	5.5	48K	29.0	827K
fr	37.1M	5.7	34K	24.6	429K
hi	17.2M	5.5	15K	21.1	281K
id	7.0M	5.2	19K	21.8	98K
ja	14.5M	5.6	24K	22.5	160K
ko	8.6M	3.9	119K	12.9	353K
pt	27.2M	5.2	32K	25.7	462K
ru	41.6M	4.7	51K	18.0	946K
zh	14.8M	6.8	20K	24.7	99K

Table 1: Basic figures describing the training datasets: number of unique patterns (N_{patt}), average number of nodes in the largest pattern in a sentence (D_{max}), number of unique lemmata ($|V|$), average number of words in a sentence (D_{words}) and total tokens in the training data (N_{tok})

would mean that there is a graph edge that hasn't been observed in the training data even on the POS level. Since this affects less than 0.2% of all generated grammars across languages, we did not implement any fallback mechanism and in these few cases our system outputs the original randomized word order for the given sentence or clause.

Finally, we use the resulting IRTG grammar to parse the UD graph and decode the string constructed by the most likely derivation. We assign identical probabilities to all rules so that the search for the most likely parse will yield the derivation with the smallest number of rules. This means that we prefer rules that connect a larger number of dependents to their head and rules that directly refer to lemmata as opposed to POS-tags. The presence of frequency counts in our model would allow us to create multiple, weighted IRTG rules for a single pattern, but exploring the effects of weighting schemes that could in some cases counteract the general preference for shorter derivations containing more specific rules is left for future work.

4 Hierarchical surface realization

Our approach to rule induction presented in the previous section yields a large number of rules. The grammar for an average sentence in the `en_ewt` dataset would contain over 1000 IRTG rules, making the parsing process prohibitively slow. We reduce the average complexity of the task by cutting UD graphs along edges that connect clauses of a sentence, thereby splitting them up into smaller graphs for which our grammar-based approach can be performed separately. The resulting word sequences can then be arranged relative to each other by performing word order restoration on the UD graph of the main clause, this time including dependents of the predicate from other clauses and interpreting them as representing their clauses. We shall now explain this method in detail and illustrate it with an example.

A simple example of an UD graph of multiple clauses, taken from the `en_ewt-ud` test set, is shown in Figure 3 and corresponds to the sentence *Click here to view it.* We begin by cutting the graph on any of the edges that may encode dependency relationships between clauses: `acl, advcl, ccomp, xcomp, conj`. In this case, the edge *click* $\xrightarrow{advcl}$ *view* is found and the graph is split into two new UD graphs that correspond to the fragments *Click here* and *view it*. What follows are three separate runs of the word order restoration algorithm described in the previous section. The first two receive as their input the UD graphs *click* $\xrightarrow{advmod}$ *here* and *view* $\xrightarrow{obj}$ *it* to determine the word order of each fragment. To arrange them with respect to each other, we run our algorithm on the UD graph *click* $\xrightarrow{advcl}$ *view*, the edge connecting the clauses, and interpret the outcome not as an order of the two words but as that of their respective clauses. This approach also enforces that non-clausal dependents of the root of a clause group together with respect to each clausal dependent, which we considered an advantage based on initial experiments with the one-step approach: arguments of a predicate separated by an intervening clause were the errors that we observed would make longer sentences entirely incomprehensible. Our algorithm is defined recursively, since a dependent clause may itself have clausal dependents. On a

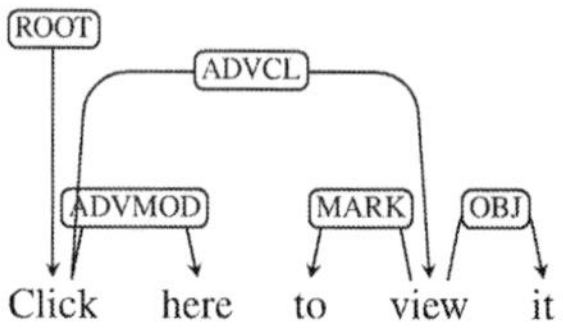

Figure 3: Sample sentence with multiple clauses

sample of 500 English sentences held out from the training dataset, we invoked the core word order restoration method 1794 times, or about 3.6 times per sentence (a single dependent clause would warrant 3 invocations). Even in such a small sample, we see one example each for recursions of depth 4, 5, and even 6, the latter caused by the following sentence (roots of clauses are marked by indices corresponding to depth): *Perhaps had we not gone*$_1$ *into this restaurant believing*$_2$ *Zahav was going*$_3$ *to be golden*$_4$ *as its name suggests*$_5$ *(and as the many golden reviews seem*$_5$ *to attest*$_6$*), we would have enjoyed*$_0$ *a decent little expensive experience.*

The reduction in average complexity of the grammars can also be illustrated using the same sample of 500 English sentences: before introducing the hierarchical approach, the 500 IRTG grammars contained more than 400 000 rules, or over 800 rules per grammar on average, resulting in an average parse time of over 4 seconds per sentence (excluding the 42 sentences for which parsing did not finish in 60 seconds, these can be parsed using a simplified grammar, see Section 5 for details). Under the clause-based approach, 1794 IRTG grammars are built to handle the 500 sentences, these contain less than 200 rules on average, and parsing time for individual clauses is just above 700 ms, which brings the per sentence parse time to 2.7 seconds. Note that we did not analyze the runtime of our entire system, these statistics are based on net parse times reported by the alto library, run on a system with 56 Intel Xeon E5-2697 v3 2.6Ghz CPUs. We expect that the greatest bottleneck in overall performance is the per-sentence generation of grammars and invocations of `alto`, but for now we chose to keep this architecture as one that makes both debugging and introspection relatively straightforward.

5 Overall architecture

Our full solution for the Surface Realization task is a pipeline of the grammar-based word order restoration system presented in Sections 3-4 and the DL-based reinflection model used in Kovács et al. (2019). For each language we begin by processing all training and test data to build a shared vocabulary for the given language, mapping lemmata to integers so that they can be represented in alto input and grammar files without the need to transform special characters. After performing the counting of subgraphs that is the training step of the grammar induction system, the model is kept in memory to efficiently serve lookup requests through a REST API to one or several instances of our tool performing word order restoration for datasets of the same language. When processing the test UD graphs, the core word order restoration algorithm is invoked for each subclause, as described in Section 4. The set of dependency edges used to split clauses is configurable and in all our experiments contained the relations `acl`, `advcl`, `ccomp`, `xcomp`, and `conj`. The IRTG rules generated are written to an alto grammar file, the UD graph is written to a file using the PENMAN notation[2], one of the formats handled by `alto`. Next, the parser is invoked as a subprocess with a configurable timeout per sentence, set to 120 seconds in our experiments. In case of a timeout, a new IRTG is generated keeping only those rules that generate subgraphs with a single edge, i.e. we retry with a much simpler grammar that can only add edges to the UD graph one-by-one. Under the clause-based approach this affected only 1% of all clauses in the test datasets. Finally, the linearized sentences are printed in the CoNLLU format and processed by the LSTM-based reinflection model trained using the parameters in Kovács et al. (2019), and a simple postprocessing step which uses simple pattern matching to detect URLs in lemmata and replaces their 'inflected' forms in the final output with the original URL. We do not perform detokenization, our final

[2]`https://penman.readthedocs.io/en/latest/notation.html`

output is the sequence of reinflected tokens separated by spaces.

6 Evaluation

The Surface Realization Shared Task uses multiple metrics for both automatic and human evaluation of system outputs. A complete presentation of all evaluations is available in Mille et al. (2020), here we present a few figures that are especially relevant to our submission. We participate in the track T1a, the closed track of the shallow surface realization task (T1). Since our method is entirely language-independent, we submitted results for all 11 languages and 35 datasets. Besides us, only the IMS team submitted outputs for languages other than English, Table 2 compare our results with theirs and with the output of the system we have extended (Kovács et al., 2019) using automatic evaluation metrics. A direct comparison with last year's system is not possible because it was trained separately for each dataset while our setup trained a single model for each language. Still, it is clear that our changes had very different effects on output quality across languages, which underlines the need for a more systematic analysis of our performance (see Section 7).

Dataset	BME-TUW 2020			BME-TUW 2019			IMS 2020		
	BLEU	NIST	DIST	BLEU	NIST	DIST	BLEU	NIST	DIST
T1_en_filtered_lines-fix	60.80	12.76	62.73	63.37	12.94	60.94	88.34	14.00	86.51
T1_es_filtered_lines-fix	61.13	13.03	57.66	16.34	10.50	35.26	87.85	14.09	87.35
T1_fr_filtered_lines-fix	46.33	11.25	58.82	51.14	11.42	66.53	89.22	13.98	91.64
T1_ko_filtered_lines-fix	53.61	11.12	62.55	40.90	10.98	49.04	76.57	11.50	80.20
T1_pt_filtered_lines-fix	42.22	10.64	59.08	11.78	9.26	34.89	83.57	13.57	84.58
T1_ru_filtered_lines-fix	51.89	12.04	56.67	13.54	10.87	33.07	77.91	12.86	82.37
T1_ar_padt-ud-test	26.00	8.29	44.78	26.40	8.29	43.06	69.56	12.63	75.80
T1_en_ewt-ud-test	57.25	12.52	65.23	59.22	12.62	62.69	86.16	13.78	88.48
T1_en_gum-ud-test	60.77	12.10	62.86	57.57	11.99	56.07	88.89	12.96	91.41
T1_en_lines-ud-test	55.98	11.78	61.44	48.78	11.54	52.77	85.05	12.98	85.89
T1_en_partut-ud-test	57.96	10.22	58.39	61.37	10.34	61.22	89.72	11.07	90.38
T1_es_ancora-ud-test	59.32	13.57	55.66	61.09	13.52	58.15	87.42	14.90	85.66
T1_es_gsd-ud-test	54.60	11.6	55.50	53.74	11.44	59.03	84.61	12.86	82.60
T1_fr_gsd-ud-test	43.21	10.41	55.48	43.80	10.33	59.35	86.08	12.58	84.64
T1_fr_partut-ud-test	52.46	9.05	62.26	49.17	8.99	56.87	87.09	10.56	85.84
T1_fr_sequoia-ud-test	45.25	10.56	57.61	46.72	10.55	59.28	87.25	12.65	85.65
T1_hi_hdtb-ud-test	57.20	11.98	57.55	63.63	12.26	64.04	84.53	13.32	83.03
T1_id_gsd-ud-test	59.16	12.14	59.62	54.22	11.82	55.57	87.53	12.89	86.41
T1_ja_gsd-ud-test	50.89	10.08	60.57	49.53	9.99	57.03	89.36	12.53	87.00
T1_ko_gsd-ud-test	58.37	12.12	66.14	46.08	11.98	52.10	81.14	12.44	85.49
T1_ko_kaist-ud-test	57.05	12.77	62.88	47.23	12.65	50.90	79.96	13.18	84.52
T1_pt_bosque-ud-test	39.89	9.89	55.63	39.53	9.77	58.72	82.92	12.40	84.59
T1_pt_gsd-ud-test	30.68	8.97	53.49	30.39	8.85	54.93	80.59	13.33	87.86
T1_ru_gsd-ud-test	54.28	11.90	53.78	54.58	11.91	52.67	77.43	12.40	78.89
T1_ru_syntagrus-ud-test	54.79	14.17	56.72	50.91	13.80	55.6	81.82	15.45	83.02
T1_zh_gsd-ud-test	50.58	11.62	54.56	58.72	11.85	59.29	86.36	12.86	83.89
T1_en_pud-ud-test	58.67	12.48	61.85	60.42	12.60	59.84	85.37	13.41	85.75
T1_ja_pud-ud-test	51.08	10.34	55.77	53.65	10.56	56.72	88.88	13.20	85.67
T1_ru_pud-ud-test	46.07	11.26	56.17	10.15	9.64	32.08	69.07	11.85	82.40
T1_en_ewt-Pred-HIT-edit	55.50	12.36	62.82	58.07	12.49	60.36	84.72	13.61	86.65
T1_en_pud-Pred-LATTICE	54.76	12.27	59.93	53.46	12.29	56.13	79.74	13.16	82.19
T1_es_ancora-Pred-HIT	59.70	13.57	56.14	61.26	13.51	58.38	86.97	14.81	86.96
T1_hi_hdtb-Pred-HIT	56.83	11.97	57.43	64.27	12.29	64.58	84.42	13.31	83.52
T1_ko_kaist-Pred-HIT	56.74	12.77	62.31	46.72	12.63	50.16	81.01	13.22	85.36
T1_pt_bosque-Pred-Stanford	41.86	9.89	56.60	40.42	9.73	59.72	84.35	12.40	87.35

Table 2: Automatic evaluation on all languages and datasets. See Mille et al. (2020) for a more detailed presentation and methodology.

Other participants submitted solutions only for a subset of the 8 English datasets, Table 3 shows results of human evaluation on the two datasets for which outputs were available from all 2020 participants. It is clear that according to these figures our system is well behind all other participants. Finally, Table 4 compares our system with the 2019 system that it extends, based on human evaluation on 6 datasets.

For each dataset, system outputs were scored on both their readability and their semantic similarity to the reference sentences. On the Russian and Spanish out-of-domain datasets derived from Wikipedia, our system significantly outperforms the original submission of Kovács et al. (2019) according to both metrics.

Team	Meaning				Readability			
	ewt		wiki		ewt		wiki	
	Ave.	Ave. z	Ave.	Ave. z	Ave.	Ave. z	Ave.	Ave. z
HUMAN					75.7	0.417	87.4	0.592
IMS	92.7	0.534	92.3	0.475	73.9	0.374	82.1	0.383
ADAPT	90.7	0.476	91.6	0.441	72.5	0.320	81.5	0.373
Concordia	87.0	0.332	88.7	0.275	70.2	0.270	79.6	0.401
BME 2020	79.3	0.086	81.8	-0.050	58.2	-0.152	60.8	-0.299
BME 2019	77.4	0.024	82.4	-0.074	56.7	-0.208	64.4	-0.181

Table 3: Human evaluation of 2020 submissions on two English datasets of the T1a track. We list average scores (Ave) and average standardized scores (Ave. z) for both meaning similarity and readability evaluations, see Mille et al. (2020) for more evaluation details.

Data	Meaning				Readability			
	BME 2020		BME 2019		BME 2020		BME 2019	
	Ave.	Ave. z	Ave.	Ave. z	Ave.	Ave. z	Ave.	Ave. z
en_ewt	79.3	0.086	77.4	0.024	58.2	-0.152	56.7	-0.208
en_wiki	81.8	-0.050	82.4	-0.074	60.8	-0.299	64.4	**-0.181**
ru_syn	81.2	-0.166	81.3	-0.177	69.7	-0.166	67.3	-0.230
ru_wiki	78.2	**-0.079**	68.2	-0.493	63.2	**0.050**	37.7	-0.781
es_ancora	70.2	-0.276	70.6	-0.271	66.4	-0.401	67.1	-0.378
es_wiki	69.8	**-0.170**	55.5	-0.726	77.2	**0.015**	62.2	-0.628

Table 4: Human evaluation of our system and the 2019 submission of Kovács et al. (2019) for all datasets. We list average scores (Ave) and average standardized scores (Ave. z) for both meaning similarity and readability evaluations. Bold figures indicate a system that significantly outperforms the other on the given metric. See Mille et al. (2020) for more evaluation details.

7 Conclusion and future work

We have presented a modification of a language-independent Surface Realization system with a fully rule-based component for word order restoration. Our main contribution is a new mechanism for generating mappings between graph and string operations using IRTG grammars that choose for a word and its dependencies the most specific patterns observed in the training data. Unlike the original system, our solution makes little use of rule weights, their sole function is currently to ensure that shorter derivations for a UD graph are preferred over longer ones. We believe that our method may be improved by introducing non-determinism in the generated grammars via some weighting scheme that allows seemingly non-optimal patterns to be chosen over those that were observed most frequently. Given the large number of parameters of our system, we also suggest the use of additional, silver-standard training data, which would be available in virtually unlimited quantities for all languages for which a high quality UD parser is available. Finally, the most important next step should be the thorough quantitative and qualitative analysis of the performance gap between our method for word order restoration and that of the state-of-the-art. Observing and quantifying correct and incorrect decisions of the grammar and updating the induction mechanism accordingly is what we consider the greatest potential of our rule-based and thus fully explainable solution.

Acknowledgements

We thank our three anynomous reviewers for the many helpful comments and suggestions. Project partly supported by BRISE-Vienna (UIA04-081), a European Union Urban Innovative Actions project. Á.K. and A.K. were partially supported by 2018-1.2.1-NKP-00008: Exploring the Mathematical Foundations of Artificial Intelligence. J.Á. was partially supported by the Hungarian Scientific Research Fund (OTKA), contract number 120145 and by the Hungarian Artificial Intelligence National Laboratory.

References

Bruno Courcelle and Joost Engelfriet. 2012. *Graph structure and monadic second-order logic*. Cambridge University Press.

Wenchao Du and Alan W Black. 2019. Learning to order graph elements with application to multilingual surface realization. In *Proceedings of the 2nd Workshop on Multilingual Surface Realisation (MSR 2019)*, pages 18–24, Hong Kong, China, November. Association for Computational Linguistics.

Johannes Gontrum, Jonas Groschwitz, Alexander Koller, and Christoph Teichmann. 2017. Alto: Rapid prototyping for parsing and translation. In *Proceedings of the Software Demonstrations of the 15th Conference of the European Chapter of the Association for Computational Linguistics*, pages 29–32.

Alexander Koller and Marco Kuhlmann. 2011. A generalized view on parsing and translation. In *Proceedings of the 12th International Conference on Parsing Technologies (IWPT)*, Dublin.

Alexander Koller. 2015. Semantic construction with graph grammars. In *Proceedings of the 14th International Conference on Computational Semantics (IWCS)*, London.

Ádám Kovács, Evelin Ács, Judit Ács, Andras Kornai, and Gábor Recski. 2019. BME-UW at SRST-2019: Surface realization with interpreted regular tree grammars. In *Proceedings of the 2nd Workshop on Multilingual Surface Realisation (MSR 2019)*, pages 35–40, Hong Kong, China. Association for Computational Linguistics.

Simon Mille, Anja Belz, Bernd Bohnet, Yvette Graham, and Leo Wanner. 2019. The Second Multilingual Surface Realisation Shared Task (SR'19): Overview and Evaluation Results. In *Proceedings of the 2nd Workshop on Multilingual Surface Realisation (MSR), 2019 Conference on Empirical Methods in Natural Language Processing (EMNLP)*, Hong Kong, China.

Simon Mille, Anya Belz, Bernd Bohnet, Thiago Castro Ferreira, Yvette Graham, and Leo Wanner. 2020. The third multilingual surface realisation shared task (SR'20): Overview and evaluation results. In *Proceedings of the 3rd Workshop on Multilingual Surface Realisation (MSR 2020)*, Dublin, Ireland. Association for Computational Linguistics.

Xiang Yu, Agnieszka Falenska, Marina Haid, Ngoc Thang Vu, and Jonas Kuhn. 2019. IMSurReal: IMS at the surface realization shared task 2019. In *Proceedings of the 2nd Workshop on Multilingual Surface Realisation (MSR 2019)*, pages 50–58, Hong Kong, China, November. Association for Computational Linguistics.

ADAPT at SR'20: How Preprocessing and Data Augmentation Help to Improve Surface Realization

Henry Elder
ADAPT Centre
Dublin City University
henry.elder@adaptcentre.ie

Abstract

In this paper, we describe the ADAPT submission to the Surface Realization Shared Task 2020. We present a neural-based system trained on the English Web Treebank and an augmented dataset, automatically created from existing text corpora.

1 Introduction

Surface realization is the final step of an NLG system (Reiter and Dale, 2000). The prior steps provide guidance on the content and structure of a sentence that is to be generated. The goal of this shared task is to generate sentences from structured data with high accuracy (Mille et al., 2020). Once this goal has been achieved, we believe neural-based surface realization systems could be incorporated into real-world NLG systems, such as task-oriented dialogue systems (Balakrishnan et al., 2019) and personalised marketing systems[1]

2 System Description

We made a submission to the Surface Realization Shared Task 2020, for the English language dataset: Universal Dependencies English Web Treebank (Silveira et al., 2014). We use a neural-based system; a sequence-to-sequence model trained on linearized trees. We submitted test outputs to both the open and closed tracks. For the open track we trained the same system on a large augmented dataset.

2.1 Data Preprocessing

Ablation analysis performed on our previous systems (Elder and Hokamp, 2018; Elder et al., 2020) showed that much of the performance comes from different preprocessing steps we apply to the original CoNLLU formatted data.

Figure 1 contains a formatted example of a linearized tree that is used as the input sequence when training the model. The output sequence used is the tokenized form of the original sentence. Below, we discuss the four key preprocessing features we use. More details can be found in the Python module used for preprocessing[2]; for each feature we point to the relevant lines of code in footnotes.

Depth First Linearizations To get the input sequence from a tree, we perform a depth first search of the tree[3]. This provides us with a linear sequence of tokens. Where a parent token has multiple child tokens, we choose randomly between the children. To ensure our system is robust to the order of the linearization, we obtain multiple random linearizations of each sentence to train the system with.

[1]For example https://phrasee.co/ and https://www.persado.com/

[2]https://github.com/Henry-E/surface-realization-shallow-task/blob/master/modules/create_source_and_target.py

[3]https://github.com/Henry-E/surface-realization-shallow-task/blob/master/modules/create_source_and_target.py\#L12-L36

Proceedings of the Third Workshop on Multilingual Surface Realisation (MSR'20), pages 30–34
Barcelona, Spain (Online), December 12, 2020.

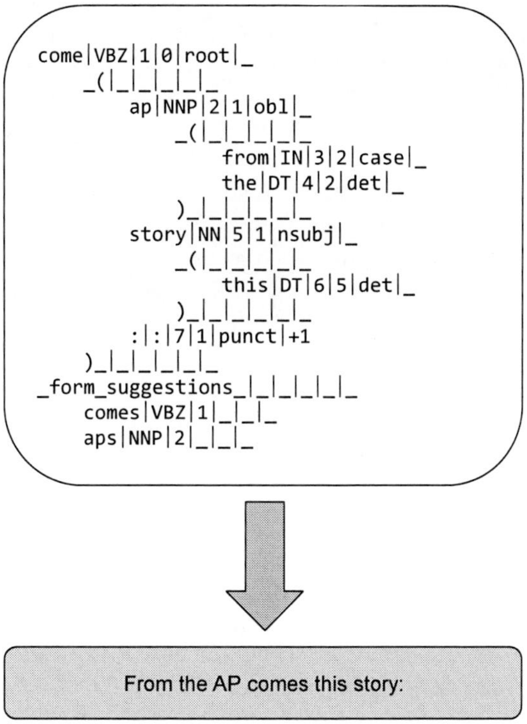

Figure 1: A formatted example of the linear input sequence for the sentence *From the AP comes this story:*. Token level features appear in the order: Lemma, XPOS, ID, Head, DepRel, Lin.

Scoping Brackets Similar to Konstas et al. (2017), we apply scoping brackets around child nodes. This provides further indication of the tree structure to the model, despite using a linear sequence as input[4].

Token Level Features We append a number of features to each token; XPOS, ID, HEAD, DepRel, Lin. This enables us to use factored sequence models (Sennrich and Haddow, 2016), which we will discuss in Section 2.3. To use this modelling feature a special pipe symbol, |, is required between each of the token's features[5].

Form Suggestions Finally, we address the problem of generating a token's form when only given its lemma. To do this, we provide the model with form suggestions[6]. Form suggestions are a list of possible forms that other lemmas, with the same XPOS tag, were observed to take. To obtain the form suggestions, we use the automatically parsed corpus, discussed in Section 2.2, to create a dictionary[7]. The dictionary is structured as such: each key is a concatenated lemma and XPOS tag, and the value is a list of possible forms observed in the automatically parsed corpus[8]. For example: {*"VBN_bootstrap": "bootstrapped"*}

2.2 Augmented Dataset

To augment the existing training data we create a dataset by parsing sentences from publicly available corpora. The two corpora we investigated are Wikitext 103 (Merity et al., 2017) and the CNN stories

[4] https://github.com/Henry-E/surface-realization-shallow-task/blob/master/modules/create_source_and_target.py\#L23-L28

[5] https://github.com/Henry-E/surface-realization-shallow-task/blob/master/modules/create_source_and_target.py\#L79-L95

[6] https://github.com/Henry-E/surface-realization-shallow-task/blob/master/modules/create_source_and_target.py\#L101-L123

[7] https://github.com/Henry-E/surface-realization-shallow-task/blob/master/modules/get_form_suggestions.py

[8] Dictionary: https://github.com/Henry-E/surface-realization-shallow-task/blob/master/inflection_dicts/18th_october_tests/lemma_form_dict_sorted.json

portion of the DeepMind Q&A dataset (Hermann et al., 2015).

Each corpus requires some cleaning and formatting, after which they can be sentence tokenized using CoreNLP (Manning et al., 2014). Sentences are filtered by length – min 5 tokens and max 50 – and for vocabulary overlap with the original training data – set to 80% of tokens in a sentence required to appear in the original vocabulary. These sentences are then parsed using the Stanford NLP UD parser (Qi et al., 2018). This leaves us with 2.4 million parsed sentences from the CNN stories corpus and 2.1 million from Wikitext. To convert a parse tree into the shared task format: word order information is removed by shuffling the IDs of the parse tree and tokens are lemmatised by removing the form column.

While it has been noted that the use of automatically created data is problematic in NLG tasks — WeatherGov (Liang et al., 2009) being the notable example — our data is created differently. The WeatherGov dataset is constructed by pairing a table with the output of a rule-based NLG system. This means any system trained on WeatherGov only re-learns the rules used to generate the text. Our approach is the reverse; we parse an existing, naturally occurring sentence, and, thus, the model must learn to reverse the parsing algorithm.

2.3 Model

The system is trained using a custom fork[9] of the OpenNMT-py framework (Klein et al., 2017), the only change made was to the beam search decoding code. The model used is a bidirectional recurrent neural network (BRNN) (Schuster and Paliwal, 1997) with long short term memory (LSTM) cells (Hochreiter and Schmidhuber, 1997). We trained two systems; one with the EWT dataset[10] and one with both the EWT dataset and our augmented dataset[11]. Hyperparameter details and replication instructions are available in our project's repository[12], in particular in the config directory. All hyperparameters stayed the same when training with the augmented dataset, except for vocabulary size and training time. Vocabulary size varies based on the datasets in use. It is determined by using any tokens which appears 10 times or more. When training on the EWT dataset, the vocabulary size is 2,193 tokens, training is done for 38 epochs and takes about 1 hour on two Nvidia 1080 Ti GPUs. For the combined EWT, Wikitext and CNN datasets the vocabulary size is 89,233, training time increases to around 2 days, and uses 60 random linearizations of the EWT dataset and 8 of the Wikitext and CNN datasets. The best performing checkpoint on the development set is chosen for testing.

Our system uses three non-standard modelling features, each of which performs a key function for the task:

Copy Attention Copy attention (Vinyals et al., 2015; See et al., 2017) gives models the ability to copy a token directly from the source sequence to the generated text, even if that token does not appear in the source vocabulary. Vocabularies are usually limited based on available data or computational constraints, so it's likely that at least some words the model sees during testing may not have been added to the vocabulary during training.

Factored Sequence Models Factored sequence models (Sennrich and Haddow, 2016) permit token level features to be used as part of training. The key idea is to create a separate embedding representation for each feature type, and to concatenate the embeddings to each token embedding to create a dense representation[13].

Restricted Beam Search In an attempt to reduce unnecessary errors during decoding, our beam search looks at the input sequence and restricts the available vocabulary to only tokens from the input, and tokens which have not yet appeared in the output sequence. This is similar to the approach used by King and White (2018).

[9] `https://github.com/Henry-E/OpenNMT-py`

[10] EWT Only Hyperparameters: `https://github.com/Henry-E/surface-realization-shallow-task/blob/master/configs/srst_2020/baseline_ewt.json\#L38-L62`

[11] Augmented Data Hyperparameters: `https://github.com/Henry-E/surface-realization-shallow-task/blob/master/configs/srst_2020/all_together.json\#L43-L67`

[12] `https://github.com/Henry-E/surface-realization-shallow-task`

[13] See Elder and Hokamp (2018) for more details

	BLEU	NIST	DIST
EWT	80.4	13.47	85.5
+ Augmented Corpora	87.5	13.81	90.35

Table 1: SR'20 EWT Test set results - Automated Evaluation metrics

3 Results

In this section we report our results on the shared task. An explanation of the evaluation methodology, as well as a comparison with other participants, can be found in the shared task description paper (Mille et al., 2020).

Table 1 contains automated evaluation metrics on the EWT test set. As in previous experiments (Elder et al., 2020), we find that the augmented dataset greatly improves the performance of our system.

System	Ave.	Ave. z	n	N
EWT + Augmented Corpora	75.7	0.426	797	913
HUMAN	**75.7**	**0.417**	**669**	**1,402**
EWT	72.5	0.32	830	953

Table 2: SR'20 Test set results - Human Evaluation: Readability

System	Ave.	Ave. z	n	N
EWT + Augmented Corpora	92.6	0.54	1,698	1,931
EWT	90.7	0.476	1,685	1,914

Table 3: SR'20 Test set results - Human Evaluation: Meaning Similarity

Table 2 contains human evaluation results for the readability metric. Rather surprisingly, the readability for our system with the augmented corpora is almost equivalent to the readability of the original human text. However, the readability metric only reflects how well written the annotators deemed a sentence to be. Readability scores don't take into account whether the generated sentence has managed to capture the meaning of the original sentence.

Table 3 contains human evaluation results for the meaning similarity metric. This metric describes how successful the system has been at generating sentences with the same meaning as the original sentence. Sentences generated by the augmented corpora are on average 92.6% similar in meaning to the original sentence. While this may seem like a strong result[14], ultimately we are aiming for 100% meaning similarity in order to have a system that is reliable enough to be used with real world NLG systems.

References

Anusha Balakrishnan, Jinfeng Rao, Kartikeya Upasani, Michael White, and Rajen Subba. 2019. Constrained Decoding for Neural NLG from Compositional Representations in Task-Oriented Dialogue. In *Proceedings of the 57th Annual Meeting of the Association for Computational Linguistics*, pages 831–844, Stroudsburg, PA, USA. Association for Computational Linguistics.

Henry Elder and Chris Hokamp. 2018. Generating High-Quality Surface Realizations Using Data Augmentation and Factored Sequence Models. In *Proceedings of the First Workshop on Multilingual Surface Realisation*, pages 49–53, Stroudsburg, PA, USA. Association for Computational Linguistics.

Henry Elder, Robert Burke, Alexander O'Connor, and Jennifer Foster. 2020. Shape of Synth to Come: Why We Should Use Synthetic Data for English Surface Realization. In *Proceedings of the 58th Annual Meeting of the Association for Computational Linguistics*, pages 7465–7471, Stroudsburg, PA, USA. Association for Computational Linguistics.

[14]The highest recorded meaning similarity on the same test set in last year's shared task was 86.6% (Mille et al., 2019)

Karl Moritz Hermann, Tomas Kocisky, Edward Grefenstette, Lasse Espeholt, Will Kay, Mustafa Suleyman, and Phil Blunsom. 2015. Teaching Machines to Read and Comprehend. In C Cortes, N D Lawrence, D D Lee, M Sugiyama, and R Garnett, editors, *Advances in Neural Information Processing Systems 28*, pages 1693–1701. Curran Associates, Inc.

Sepp Hochreiter and Jurgen Schmidhuber. 1997. Long Short-Term Memory. *Neural Computation*, 9(8):1735–1780.

David King and Michael White. 2018. The OSU Realizer for SRST '18: Neural Sequence-to-Sequence Inflection and Incremental Locality-Based Linearization. In *Proceedings of the First Workshop on Multilingual Surface Realisation*, number 2009, pages 39–48, Stroudsburg, PA, USA. Association for Computational Linguistics.

Guillaume Klein, Yoon Kim, Yuntian Deng, Jean Senellart, and Alexander Rush. 2017. OpenNMT: Open-Source Toolkit for Neural Machine Translation. In *Proceedings of ACL 2017, System Demonstrations*, pages 67–72, Stroudsburg, PA, USA. Association for Computational Linguistics.

Ioannis Konstas, Srinivasan Iyer, Mark Yatskar, Yejin Choi, and Luke Zettlemoyer. 2017. Neural AMR: Sequence-to-Sequence Models for Parsing and Generation. In *Proceedings of the 55th Annual Meeting of the Association for Computational Linguistics (Volume 1: Long Papers)*, pages 146–157, Stroudsburg, PA, USA, 4. Association for Computational Linguistics.

Percy Liang, Michael I. Jordan, and Dan Klein. 2009. Learning Semantic Correspondences with Less Supervision. *Proceedings of the Joint Conference of the 47th Annual Meeting of the ACL and the 4th International Joint Conference on Natural Language Processing of the AFNLP*, (August):91–99.

Christopher D Manning, Mihai Surdeanu, John Bauer, Jenny Finkel, Steven J Bethard, and David McClosky. 2014. The {Stanford} {CoreNLP} Natural Language Processing Toolkit. In *Association for Computational Linguistics (ACL) System Demonstrations*, pages 55–60.

Stephen Merity, Caiming Xiong, James Bradbury, and Richard Socher. 2017. Pointer Sentinel Mixture Models. In *5th International Conference on Learning Representations, {ICLR} 2017, Toulon, France, April 24-26, 2017, Conference Track Proceedings*. OpenReview.net.

Simon Mille, Anja Belz, Bernd Bohnet, Yvette Graham, and Leo Wanner. 2019. The Second Multilingual Surface Realisation Shared Task (SR'19): Overview and Evaluation Results. In *Proceedings of the 2nd Workshop on Multilingual Surface Realisation (MSR 2019)*, number Msr, pages 1–17, Stroudsburg, PA, USA. Association for Computational Linguistics.

Simon Mille, Anya Belz, Bernd Bohnet, Thiago Castro Ferreira, Yvette Graham, and Leo Wanner. 2020. The Third Multilingual Surface Realisation Shared Task ({SR}{'}20): Overview and Evaluation Results. In *Proceedings of the 3nd Workshop on Multilingual Surface Realisation (MSR 2020)*, Dublin, Ireland, 12. Association for Computational Linguistics.

Peng Qi, Timothy Dozat, Yuhao Zhang, and Christopher D Manning. 2018. Universal Dependency Parsing from Scratch. In *Proceedings of the (CoNLL) 2018 Shared Task: Multilingual Parsing from Raw Text to Universal Dependencies*, pages 160–170, Brussels, Belgium, 10. Association for Computational Linguistics.

Ehud Reiter and Robert Dale. 2000. *Building Natural Language Generation Systems*. Cambridge University Press, New York, NY, USA.

M. Schuster and K.K. Paliwal. 1997. Bidirectional recurrent neural networks. *IEEE Transactions on Signal Processing*, 45(11):2673–2681.

Abigail See, Peter J. Liu, and Christopher D. Manning. 2017. Get To The Point: Summarization with Pointer-Generator Networks. In *Proceedings of the 55th Annual Meeting of the Association for Computational Linguistics (Volume 1: Long Papers)*, pages 1073–1083, Stroudsburg, PA, USA. Association for Computational Linguistics.

Rico Sennrich and Barry Haddow. 2016. Linguistic Input Features Improve Neural Machine Translation. In *Proceedings of the First Conference on Machine Translation: Volume 1, Research Papers*, pages 83–91, Stroudsburg, PA, USA. Association for Computational Linguistics.

Natalia Silveira, Timothy Dozat, Marie-Catherine de Marneffe, Samuel Bowman, Miriam Connor, John Bauer, and Chris Manning. 2014. A Gold Standard Dependency Corpus for {E}nglish. In *Proceedings of the Ninth International Conference on Language Resources and Evaluation ({LREC}'14)*, pages 2897–2904, Reykjavik, Iceland, 5. European Language Resources Association (ELRA).

Oriol Vinyals, Meire Fortunato, and Navdeep Jaitly. 2015. Pointer Networks. In *Advances in Neural Information Processing Systems 28*, pages 2692–2700, 6.

IMSurReal Too: IMS at the Surface Realization Shared Task 2020

Xiang Yu, Simon Tannert, Ngoc Thang Vu, Jonas Kuhn
Institut für Maschinelle Sprachverarbeitung
University of Stuttgart, Germany
firstname.lastname@ims.uni-stuttgart.de

Abstract

We introduce the IMS contribution to the Surface Realization Shared Task 2020. Our current system achieves substantial improvement over the state-of-the-art system from last year, mainly due to a better token representation and a better linearizer, as well as a simple ensembling approach. We also experiment with data augmentation, which brings some additional performance gain. The system is available at https://github.com/EggplantElf/IMSurReal.

1 Introduction

This paper presents our submission to the Surface Realization Shared Task 2020 (Mille et al., 2020). As in the previous year, we participate in both the shallow and the deep track. Additionally, we also participate in the new setting, where additional unlabeled data is permitted to train the models.

Since last year's SR'19 shared task (Mille et al., 2019), we have made some improvements over the winning system, mostly described in Yu et al. (2020). In particular, we designed a new linearization module, where we cast the task of word ordering as a Traveling Salesman Problem (TSP), and use the biaffine attention model (Dozat and Manning, 2016) to calculate the score. The new linearizer greatly reduces the decoding time and improves the performance. We also addressed a problem in the previous system which restricted the output to projective trees by employing a transition-based reordering system, which is inspired by transition-based non-projective parsing (Nivre, 2009).

Inspired by the large improvement from data augmentation in Elder et al. (2020), we utilize extra training data for all languages. We parse unlabeled sentences from news and Wikipedia text, then convert the parse trees into the shared task format, and train our system on the augmented data.

Finally, we apply simple ensembling by majority voting using ten models to improve the stability of the system and further push towards the performance upper bound.

2 Surface Realization System

Our system largely follows our submission from the previous year (Yu et al., 2019), with some major change in the linearization module. It consists of up to five modules working in a pipeline fashion. The first module is linearization, which orders the input dependency tree (shallow or deep alike) into a sequence of lemmata. The second module is reordering, which adjusts the sequence from the previous step such that the new sequence could be non-projective. The third module is function word completion (for the deep track only), which generates function words as the dependents of the content words from the previous step. The fourth module is morphological inflection, which turns the sequence of lemmata into inflected word forms. Finally, the fifth module is contraction, which contracts several words as one token, e.g. from *de el* to *del* in Spanish.

For a more detailed description, we refer the readers to Yu et al. (2020). In this section, we mainly describe the changes we made since last year's shared task.

Proceedings of the Third Workshop on Multilingual Surface Realisation (MSR'20), pages 35–41
Barcelona, Spain (Online), December 12, 2020.

Figure 1 gives an example of the linearization process (including the reordering), which is our main contribution in this work. We first divide the input dependency tree into subtrees, and use the linearization decoder to order each subtree separately, then combine the ordered subtrees as a full projective sentence respecting the orders in the subtrees. Finally, we use a reordering system to adjust the sentence, and produce potentially non-projective sentences.

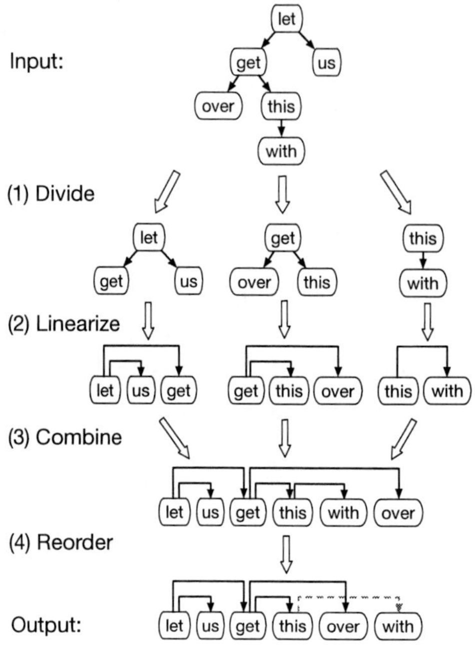

Figure 1: An overview of the linearization module.

2.1 Dependency Tree Encoding

We use the bidirectional Tree-LSTM as in Yu et al. (2019) to encode the input dependency tree. We made two changes in the encoder compared to last year. First, in addition to the default features, i.e., lemma, UPOS, morphological features, and dependency relations, we also use a character-based bidirectional LSTM to encode the lemma, so that out-of-vocabulary words can be better represented. Second, instead of concatenating the feature vectors, we sum them up with the same dimensionality, so that the token representation is more compact and the model has fewer parameters. In addition to the feature-level vectors, we also add the tree-level vectors to the overall representation. Preliminary experiments show that these changes bring substantial improvement.

We run a bidirectional LSTM on the characters in the lemma (denoted as $\mathbf{c}_0$ to $\mathbf{c}_p$) and another bidirectional LSTM for the morphological tags (denoted as $\mathbf{m}_0$ to $\mathbf{m}_q$).

$$\mathbf{v}_i^{(char)} = \overrightarrow{\text{LSTM}}^{char}(\mathbf{c}_0...\mathbf{c}_p) + \overleftarrow{\text{LSTM}}^{char}(\mathbf{c}_0...\mathbf{c}_p) \tag{1}$$

$$\mathbf{v}_i^{(morph)} = \overrightarrow{\text{LSTM}}^{morph}(\mathbf{m}_0...\mathbf{m}_q) + \overleftarrow{\text{LSTM}}^{morph}(\mathbf{m}_0...\mathbf{m}_q) \tag{2}$$

The feature-level representation is then the sum of the feature embeddings from the lemma, UPOS, and dependency relations, together with the LSTM outputs for the lemma characters and morphological tags.

$$\mathbf{v}_i^{(token)} = \mathbf{v}_i^{(lem)} + \mathbf{v}_i^{(pos)} + \mathbf{v}_i^{(dep)} + \mathbf{v}_i^{(morph)} + \mathbf{v}_i^{(char)} \tag{3}$$

We then use the Tree-LSTM as in the previous system to model the tree-level representation, and sum it with the feature-level representation, which is used as the final token representation in the linearization, reordering, and completion.

$$\mathbf{v}_i^{(tree)} = \text{Tree-LSTM}(\mathbf{v}_0^{(token)}...\mathbf{v}_n^{(token)})_i \tag{4}$$

$$\mathbf{x}_i = \mathbf{v}_i^{(token)} + \mathbf{v}_i^{(tree)} \tag{5}$$

For the inflection and contraction modules, since the token sequence is already determined, we additionally use a bidirectional LSTM to model the sequence, and the output vector is also added into the final representation.

$$\mathbf{v}_i^{(seq)} = \text{BiLSTM}(\mathbf{v}_0^{(token)}...\mathbf{v}_n^{(token)})_i \tag{6}$$

$$\mathbf{x}_i' = \mathbf{v}_i^{(token)} + \mathbf{v}_i^{(tree)} + \mathbf{v}_i^{(seq)} \tag{7}$$

2.2 Graph-based Linearization

Similar to our previous system, we take a divide-and-conquer approach by breaking each dependency tree into subtrees, consisting of a head and several dependents, and order the subtrees individually. Finally, we combine the ordered subtrees into a full sentence.

In our previous system, we used beam search to build up the sequence incrementally following Bohnet et al. (2010). It achieves good performance, however, the nature of beam search restricts the training and decoding speed, since the model has to make a calculation at every step. Instead, we use a graph-based decoding method proposed in Yu et al. (2020), in which we model the linearization task as a Traveling Salesman Problem (TSP): each word is treated as a city, the score of a bigram in the output sequence is the traveling cost from a city to another, and the optimal sequence of words is the shortest route that visits each city exactly once. In this formulation, the model only needs to calculate the costs of all the potential bigrams all at once, and an off-the-shelf TSP solver is used to find the optimal sequence. We adapt the biaffine attention model (Dozat and Manning, 2016) to calculate the bigram score, then interpret the score as the traveling cost.

First, we use two multi-layer perceptrons (MLPs) to obtain different views of the token representation as the first and second word in the bigram:

$$\mathbf{h}_i^{(fr)} = \text{MLP}^{(fr)}(\mathbf{x}_i) \tag{8}$$

$$\mathbf{h}_i^{(to)} = \text{MLP}^{(to)}(\mathbf{x}_i) \tag{9}$$

We then apply the biaffine transformation on the vectors of the first word $\mathbf{h}_i^{(fr)}$ and the second word $\mathbf{h}_j^{(to)}$ to compute the score $s_{i,j}$ of each bigram (i, j), where $\mathbf{W}$ is the weight matrix of size $(k+1)\times(k+1)$, and k is the size of $\mathbf{h}_i^{(fr)}$ and $\mathbf{h}_j^{(to)}$:

$$s_{i,j} = (\mathbf{h}_i^{(fr)} \oplus 1) \times \mathbf{W} \times (\mathbf{h}_j^{(to)} \oplus 1)^\top \tag{10}$$

In the actual computation, we parallelize Equation 10, where $\mathbf{S}$ is the output score matrix of size $n \times n$, and n is the number of tokens:

$$\mathbf{S} = (\mathbf{H}^{(fr)} \oplus \mathbf{1}) \times \mathbf{W} \times (\mathbf{H}^{(to)} \oplus \mathbf{1})^\top \tag{11}$$

Finally, we turn the score matrix into a non-negative cost matrix for the TSP solver:

$$\mathbf{C} = \max(\mathbf{S}) - \mathbf{S} \tag{12}$$

We use an off-the-shelf TSP solver, OR-Tools[1], to decode the TSP. In particular, we use a greedy decoding algorithm, which does not guarantee the optimal solution, but typically gives good results, since the TSP size is generally quite small (less than 10 tokens in each subtree).

[1] `https://developers.google.com/optimization`

2.3 Transition-based Reordering

The divide-and-conquer strategy greatly reduces the problem size, which facilitates the TSP decoding, however, it comes with the price that the output sentence is bound to be projective.

To remedy this problem, we introduce a transition system to reorder a projective sentence into a potentially non-projective one. It is essentially a simplified version of the non-projective parsing system by Nivre (2009), with only two transitions, *shift* and *swap*, as shown in Table 1.

Transition	Before		After
shift	$(\sigma,\ [i\|\beta])$	$\rightarrow$	$([\sigma\|i],\ \beta)$
swap	$([\sigma\|i],\ [j\|\beta])$	$\rightarrow$	$(\sigma,\ [j\|i\|\beta])$

Table 1: The *shift-swap* transition system.

We use two LSTMs to model the stack and buffer, then concatenate the output from the top of the stack and the front of the buffer and predict the next transition with an MLP. After each transition, the representation of the stack and the buffer will be updated.

2.4 Subsequent Modules

The subsequent modules are exactly the same as in previous year, we only very briefly describe them, and refer the reader to Yu et al. (2019) for the details.

The function word completion module takes the ordered deep dependency tree as input, and generates function words to the left and right for each content word. Only when a special symbol signifying stopping generation is predicted, we move to generate function words to the next content word.

The inflection module is similar to the hard-monotonic attention model by Aharoni and Goldberg (2017), which uses a pointer to indicate the current input character in the lemma and predicts edit operations to generate the inflected word. To increase the robustness on irregular inflection, we combine the model with a rule-based system, which takes precedence if the lemma and morphological tag combination is frequent and unique in the training data.

The contraction module has two steps. We first assign BIO tags to each word, which group the words that need to be contracted together. The grouped words are then concatenated as a sequence, and passed to a standard Seq2Seq model to generate the contracted word.

2.5 Data Augmentation

On top of the aforementioned improvements, we train our model with additional data to allow it to generalize better. To ensure maximum compatibility with the original training data, we filter large publicly available datasets according to certain criteria.

For T1 we use the automatically annotated treebanks from the CoNLL 2017 shared task[2], for T2 we use a subset of the English data from Elder et al. (2020) and for French and Spanish the freely available news datasets from webhose.io[3]. We parse each dataset with UDPipe using the official pretrained models.

In order to maximize compatibility, we filter the new datasets to be more similar to the original training data. We control for sentence length and branching factor by estimating their distributions in both the original training data and the new datasets. To be able to efficiently filter using rejection sampling, we normalize the distributions in the original training data by the maximum value to obtain probabilities between 0 and 1.

During sampling we decide if we accept or reject a sentence using the product of both probabilities as well as the ratio of old vocabulary. An example of the result of filtering can be seen in Figure 2.

$$\mathrm{p}(s) = \mathbf{D_1}(s) * \mathbf{D_2}(s) * \frac{||v_{original} \cap v_s||}{||v_s||} \tag{13}$$

[2]https://lindat.mff.cuni.cz/repository/xmlui/handle/11234/1-1989

[3]https://webhose.io/free-datasets/language/

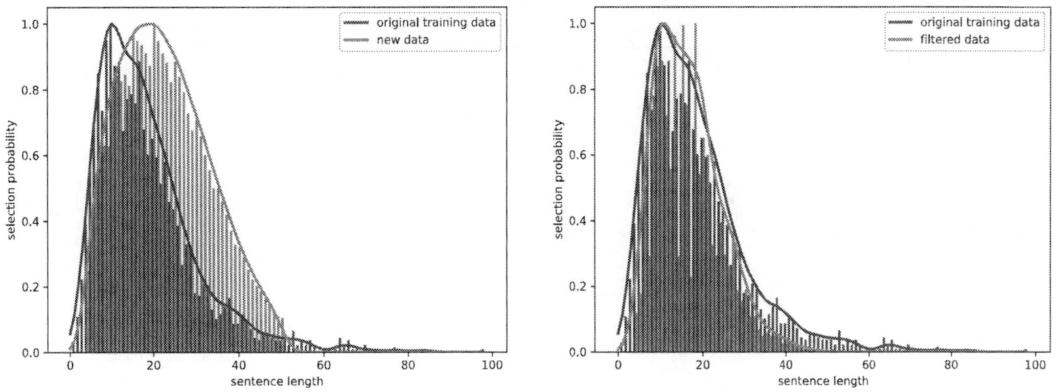

(a) Distributions of the original data in blue and the new data before filtering in red.

(b) Distribution of the original data in blue and the new data after filtering in red.

Figure 2: Sentence length distribution in *en_lines* before and after filtering

We sample 200,000 sentences for each treebank and convert them into the shared task format as extra training data, which is only used to train the linearization and function word completion modules, since it did not show significant improvement for other modules. The amount of data is rather small compared the 4.5 million sentences in Elder et al. (2020). We also experimented with 1 million sentences, but the improvement was slightly smaller than with 200,000 sentences, the exact reason is yet to be determined.

2.6 Ensembling

We apply a simple ensembling method to further push the performance. We train 10 instances of each module with the same hyperparameters but different random seed, and use majority voting to select the final output sentence. On the development sets, the ensemble prediction performs about 1 BLEU point higher than the single model on average.

For the open track, we train multiple models with different ratios between the original and the augmented data. Concretely, after training one step with the original data, we train N steps with the augmented data, where N ranges from 1 to 10. For different treebanks, the optimal value of N varies drastically, we simply take the majority prediction from these ten models.

2.7 Hyperparameters

For simplicity, we use the same dimensionality of 128 for all the components in the model, including the embeddings, LSTMs, MLPs. All LSTMs have only one layer, and all MLPs have two layers. The total number of parameters range from 1 to 8 millions, mainly depending on the vocabulary size, which is capped at 50,000. We use the Adam optimizer (Kingma and Ba, 2014) with the default parameters for training, and when the model stops improving, we switch to simple stochastic gradient descent to continue training until it again stops improving. No mini-batch or dropout are used during training, as they did not show improvements in the preliminary experiments. The model is implemented with the CPU version of DyNet[4], which takes several hours to train on a single CPU core.

3 Evaluation

This year, we are the only team to submit predictions on all the tracks and languages. The average BLEU scores in the shallow and deep tracks for last year and this year's closed and open subtracks are listed in Table 2, while the detailed evaluations are reported in Mille et al. (2020).

In the closed subtrack, our system improves over the previous year by 3.59 points in T1 and 2.68 points in T2. The improvement mainly comes from a better token representation, a better linearizer, and the model ensembling. In the open subtrack, the augmented data brings an additional gain of 0.49 in T1

[4] `http://dynet.io/`

	2019	2020a	2020b
T1	80.17	83.76	84.25
T2	51.60	54.28	55.76
T1 ∩ T2	84.24	86.53	86.88

Table 2: Comparing the average BLEU scores of our SR'19 results with this year's closed (2020a) and open (2020b) subtrack.

and 1.48 in T2. When we consider only the subset of T1 treebanks that also appear in T2 (T1 ∩ T2), the gain of the additional data is only 0.35. It is clear that the additional training data are more beneficial for the T2 track, since the function word completion module requires more training data. However, the improvement of augmented data in our system is much smaller compared with the ADAPT team which only submitted results for English. This suggests that there is still room for improvement for applying data augmentation in our system.

In the human evaluation, our systems (with or without data augmentation) come in second place for English in terms of meaning similarity and readability, and first for Russian and Spanish.

4 Conclusion

In this paper, we describe our submission to the SR'20 shared task, which is based on our system in SR'19, with some improvements in the feature representation and the linearization module. Additionally, we augment the training data with parsed news and Wikipedia texts. The results show that the additional data can improve the performance to some extent, especially in the deep track, but not as prominent as in Elder et al. (2020). More careful analysis and design are thus required for the augmentation as well as the training process in order to fully capitalize on the vast amount of unlabeled data.

Acknowledgements

Xiang Yu is supported by the Ministry of Science, Research and the Arts of the State of Baden-Württemberg (MWK), within the CLARIN-D research project. Simon Tannert is supported by IBM Research AI through the IBM AI Horizons Network.

References

Roee Aharoni and Yoav Goldberg. 2017. Morphological Inflection Generation with Hard Monotonic Attention. In *Proceedings of the 55th Annual Meeting of the Association for Computational Linguistics (Volume 1: Long Papers)*, pages 2004–2015.

Bernd Bohnet, Leo Wanner, Simon Mille, and Alicia Burga. 2010. Broad Coverage Multilingual Deep Sentence Generation with a Stochastic Multi-Level Realizer. In *Proceedings of the 23rd International Conference on Computational Linguistics*, pages 98–106. Association for Computational Linguistics.

Timothy Dozat and Christopher D. Manning. 2016. Deep Biaffine Attention for Neural Dependency Parsing. *ArXiv*, abs/1611.01734.

Henry Elder, Robert Burke, Alexander O'Connor, and Jennifer Foster. 2020. Shape of synth to come: Why we should use synthetic data for English surface realization. In *Proceedings of the 58th Annual Meeting of the Association for Computational Linguistics*, pages 7465–7471, Online, July. Association for Computational Linguistics.

Diederik P Kingma and Jimmy Ba. 2014. Adam: A method for stochastic optimization. *arXiv preprint arXiv:1412.6980*.

Simon Mille, Anja Belz, Bernd Bohnet, Yvette Graham, and Leo Wanner. 2019. The Second Multilingual Surface Realisation Shared Task (SR'19): Overview and Evaluation Results. In *Proceedings of the 2nd Workshop on Multilingual Surface Realisation (MSR), 2019 Conference on Empirical Methods in Natural Language Processing (EMNLP)*, Hong Kong, China.

Simon Mille, Anya Belz, Bernd Bohnet, Thiago Castro Ferreira, Yvette Graham, and Leo Wanner. 2020. The third multilingual surface realisation shared task (SR'20): Overview and evaluation results. In *Proceedings of the 3nd Workshop on Multilingual Surface Realisation (MSR 2020)*, Dublin, Ireland, December. Association for Computational Linguistics.

Joakim Nivre. 2009. Non-Projective Dependency Parsing in Expected Linear Time. In *Proceedings of the Joint Conference of the 47th Annual Meeting of the ACL and the 4th International Joint Conference on Natural Language Processing of the AFNLP*, pages 351–359, Suntec, Singapore, August. Association for Computational Linguistics.

Xiang Yu, Agnieszka Falenska, Marina Haid, Ngoc Thang Vu, and Jonas Kuhn. 2019. IMSurReal: IMS at the Surface Realization Shared Task 2019. In *Proceedings of the 2nd Workshop on Multilingual Surface Realisation (MSR 2019)*, pages 50–58, Hong Kong, China, November. Association for Computational Linguistics.

Xiang Yu, Simon Tannert, Ngoc Thang Vu, and Jonas Kuhn. 2020. Fast and accurate non-projective dependency tree linearization. In *Proceedings of the 58th Annual Meeting of the Association for Computational Linguistics*, pages 1451–1462, Online, July. Association for Computational Linguistics.

Lexical Induction of Morphological and Orthographic Forms for Low-Resourced Languages

Taha Tobaili
Knowledge Media Institute
The Open University
taha.tobaili@open.ac.uk

Abstract

Languages with large vocabularies pose a challenge for lexical induction especially if they are too low in resources to train sophisticated language models. The situation becomes even more challenging if the language lacks a standard orthography, such that spelling variants cannot be referenced with a standard format for lexical simplification. We propose a simple approach to induce morphological and orthographic forms in low-resourced NLP and prove its potential on a non-standard language as a use case.

1 Introduction

A language is considered to have a high degree of lexical sparsity if the words of the language could have a high number of forms (Baly et al., 2017), whether morphological (inflections) or orthographic (spellings). As a result the number of possible forms for many words becomes large, a considerable challenge in NLP for low-resourced languages. With the lack of linguistic resources, several NLP tasks become difficult to achieve such as named entity recognition (NER), part of speech (POS) tagging, parsing, question answering (QA), machine translation (MT), and sentiment analysis.

Stemming, lemmatisation, and normalisation of text are the most intuitive text preprocessing tasks to address a highly-sparsed language[1], with the goal of simplifying a variety of word forms into one standard form, such that the inflected or differently-spelled forms match easily with their lemmas or roots in a lexicon or corpus. On the other hand, it reduces the number of word forms in a dataset to train a machine learning (ML) algorithm. As plausible as this direction sounds, it is not as straightforward for morphologically-rich languages (MRLs) as it is for languages with simple morphology. In English for example, the words *enjoyed, enjoying, enjoyable, joyful, and unjoyful* can easily map with the lexemes *enjoy* and *joy*. In Arabic however, the inflections are not limited to prefixes and suffixes but also include infixes, proclitics, and enclitics. The affixes consist of objects and pronouns that are tense, number, and gender sensitive as well, that one verb could easily expand to a hundred inflectional forms. Arabic is also rich in tri-literal words because of the short vowel diacritic transcript, as such even a slight inflection could map with a list of irrelevant words, for example: استنكار (*denying*) maps with eleven words of different meanings سكر نكر نار تنكر تنك كر سار تار ستار ستر استنار.

Mapping words with their base forms becomes even more difficult when the language is purely spoken, lacking a standard orthography. Thus, if transcribed, people spell words according to their own perception of how phonemes should be represented in text, resulting in various spellings for each word.

In this work, we choose Arabizi (Yaghan, 2008), an informal heuristic transcription of the spoken dialectal Arabic (DA) in Latin script. A language that poses both issues, rich morphology and inconsistent orthography. Not only can each word be inflected into many forms, but also each form could be written in a variety of ways. Hence, the magnitude of its lexical sparsity quickly becomes very large as it is a multiple of its morphology and orthography.

[1]A language with a high degree of lexical sparsity.

Proceedings of the Third Workshop on Multilingual Surface Realisation (MSR'20), pages 42–49
Barcelona, Spain (Online), December 12, 2020.

Unlike the formal Modern Standard Arabic (MSA), the spoken vernacular DA is quiet esoteric to different regions with different structure, word choice, vocabulary, conjugation, speech tempo, and pronunciation. It is influenced by other languages as well such as French, Turkish, Spanish, or Italian based on the history of the region. We focus on the Lebanese dialect Arabizi as the use case of this study, a member of the larger Levantine dialect family with less resources in the literature than Egyptian, North-African, or Gulf dialects. The Lebanese dialect is also known for its mixing with English and French which is also reflected in its Arabizi transcription (Sullivan, 2017; Tobaili, 2016), another challenge for word classification.

We address the problem of the large lexical sparsity of Arabizi by taking a reversed approach; rather than attempting to lemmatise or simplify words, we retrieve a high number of written forms for given input words from a raw corpus. We propose an approach that combines rule-based mapping with word embeddings to automatically expand Arabizi words. We test this approach on a lexicon composed of 2K sentiment words that resulted in a new sentiment lexicon of 175K words. We evaluate the approach extrinsically by testing the newly expanded sentiment lexicon against a pre-annotated Arabizi dataset.

As such, the contributions of this work are mainly an approach to find the written forms of words in highly-sparsed low-resourced languages and the outcome resource, a new Lebanese dialect Arabizi sentiment lexicon.

2 Related Work

In this work we build upon our previous work of (Tobaili et al., 2019), where we compiled a raw corpus and developed a new sentiment lexicon and datasets for the Lebanese dialect Arabizi. We started by developing a 2K sentiment words lexicon and followed by expanding it using the cosine word similarity feature, nearest neighbours, from an embedding space trained on the raw corpus. This yielded in a lexicon of 24.6K words, named SenZi, an average of 12 forms per word, to cover some inflectional and orthographic variants of the original sentiment words.

However, the degree of the lexical sparsity in Arabizi is higher than 12 variants per word as can be seen in Section 4. We therefore, propose a new approach that expanded the same 2K sentiment words into 175K words using a rule-based technique to match with variants, or forms, from that same corpus. We also utilise the cosine word similarity feature of the embeddings, not to retrieve words, but to associate the new words with sentiment scores and disambiguate them after the expansion.

In (Soricut and Och, 2015), the authors generated morphological inflections computationally by adding prefixes and suffixes to a set of vocabulary. They then measured the cosine similarity of each original word with the generated form to evaluate the morphological generation. Although this work is similar in concept to our work, the complexity of Arabic morphology is beyond simple prefixes and suffixes as mentioned in Section 1, hence we do not transform the vocabulary by adding affixes, rather we map the structure of that vocabulary with words of similar structure in the corpus. Similarly, we measure the cosine word similarity to rank the retrieved forms.

Other works considered the non-standard orthographies, such as the texts found on social media, a noisy or ill forms of the correct standard languages, thus emphasised their efforts on matching the equivalent forms of the noisy text with that of the standard orthography. For example, (Han and Baldwin, 2011) developed a classifier to detect the noisy forms, then generated correction candidate words based on the morphophonemic similarity. (Contractor et al., 2010) replaced the noisy words with a list of possible regular forms in a given set of sentences, then maximised the product of the weighted list and language model scores to generate cleaner versions of these sentences. (Gouws et al., 2011) used an unsupervised approach to extract word variants, in pairs, from domain specific corpora. They computed the distributional similarity among all word pairs in a domain specific corpus, filtered the common English ones, and scored the relation of the pairs using their semantic and lexical similarities. (Derczynski et al., 2013) also tried to automatically replace noisy words with standard English equivalents. Similar works presented in the (Baldwin et al., 2015) shared task on noisy user-generated text, where the participants were specifically asked to convert non-standard words to their standard forms for English tweets.

Most of these works considered that a correct form of the noisy words exist, therefore perceived the task as finding the best word replacement, similar in concept to text simplification (Nisioi et al., 2017) which aims at transforming original words into simpler variants. This is similar to our problem except that there is no correct or wrong way to transcribe a spoken language that lacks a standard orthography, such as Arabizi; for that, our goal is to find all possible morphological and orthographic forms, for any given word, that are naturally written in text. The issue of non-standard orthography is not limited to Arabizi, but to many spoken languages and dialects (Millour and Fort, 2020), we therefore aspire that our contribution spans across other such languages as well.

3 Background and Challenges

Arabizi scripture contains several linguistic complexities that it is even called hell in (Seddah et al., 2020). We now scrutinise the transcription of Arabizi to explain how these complexities came to exist.

First of all, because dialectal Arabic (DA) is spoken, in its nature it lacks a consensus on an orthography, for that transcribing Arabic phonemes in a script of different languages (Latin) heuristically widens the orthographic inconsistency even further for the reasons summed below.

1. A word is transcribed based on how it is pronounced, hence different pronunciations of the same word spell differently. For example, the one letter vowel phoneme ي /yā/ in the positive word خير (*fine*) is pronounced as /āy/ khāyr or /eh/ kher, therefore both *khayr* and *kher* are common transcriptions for the same word.

2. There is no consistency in transcribing vowel phonemes. Both *khāyr* and *kher* could be transcribed as *kher, kheir, khair, kheyr, khayr,* or even without most vowel letters such as *khyr.*

3. There is little consistency in transcribing distinct consonant phonemes, such as the guttural ح ā', خ Khā', ع ayn, غ Ghayn that articulate in the post-velar areas of the oral cavity and the glottal stop ء Hamzah. For example, the خ Khā' in the mentioned word خير *khāyr* is standardised to some extent as compound letters *kh* or numeral 5 or even 7'. As such, all the following are possible orthographies for this tri-literal base word: *kher, kheir, khair, kheyr, khayr, khyr, 5er, 5eir, 5air, 5eyr, 5ayr, 5yr, 7'er, 7'eir, 7'air, 7'eyr, 7'ayr, 7'yr.* Note that different regions adopted different standards.

4. Finally, switching between Arabic and English or French is normal in DA speech. This is reflected in Arabizi texting as well, known as codeswitching (Aboelezz, 2009).

Additionally, transcribing a high number of phonemes into lower number of letters generates word ambiguity and causes Arabizi words to overlap with English words. However, in this work we focus on addressing the sparsity challenge.

This large lexical sparsity of Arabizi is even faced with a severe lack of resources. The existing corpus of 53MB Lebanese dialect Arabizi (Tobaili et al., 2019) is considered insufficient to train powerful data-hungry language models such as BERT and GPT (Devlin et al., 2018; Radford et al., 2018); a fundamental challenge for low-resourced languages.

On another note, attempting to convert Arabizi to Lebanese Arabic script, similar to the sophisticated works of (Darwish, 2014; Al-Badrashiny et al., 2014; Guellil et al., 2017; Masmoudi et al., 2019), serves us no purpose for lexical induction. We simply exploit the existing corpus to maximise the forms of given words using a rule-based combined with word embeddings approach.

4 Approach

We use the datasets that we previously created in (Tobaili et al., 2019) to test and evaluate the proposed approach. Briefly, we developed an Arabizi sentiment lexicon of 2K words, composed of 600 positive and 1.4K negative words separately, and expanded it to 24.6K words using the cosine word similarity feature of word embeddings trained on a corpus of 1M Facebook comments. We evaluated the lexicon using a simple lexicon-based approach against a sentiment-annotated dataset of 1.6K Arabizi tweets.

We now propose to expand that original sentiment lexicon (2K words) through several steps. We first normalise the text and search the entire Facebook corpus for all words matching the structure of the lexicon words under a linguistic constraint of permitted affix letters. We follow by adding cosine word similarity scores obtained from the word embeddings between every matched word and the original lexicon word to use it as a sentiment score and disambiguate forms that are retrieved in both positive and negative lists. We detail each step below.

1. **Normalisation:** Since transcribing consonant letters is standardised to a low extent in Arabizi as shown in Section 3, we normalise all observed compound letters that represent consonant phonemes with single numerals or symbols of a similar grapheme: (ch or sh ش with $), (gh غ with 8), and (kh خ with 5). The phonemes of ذ ظ , and ث are pronounced as *z* and *s* in the Lebanese dialect, hence normalised by nature. We also reduce repeated consonant letters down to one letter in exaggerated words: *habibbbi* to *habibi*.

   We apply this normalisation to determine which words to match only. If there is a match, we retrieve the word in its original un-normalised format.

2. **Matching:** We match the consonant letter sequence (CLS) of each lexicon word with all words containing the same sequence in the corpus: *fa5r* (*pride*) (f5r) matches with *fakhour, fakher, fa5er, fa5eir, fakhooorrr* after normalisation.

   If more consonant letters precede or follow the sequence, we check if these letters fall within a predefined set of observed prefixes (*2 l s w t b y m n*) and suffixes (*k l t n h w y*): *fa5r* (f5r) matches with all the following inflections *benfe5r, mntfekhar, fakhourin, fa5rna, fakhourah* because the prefixes *b, m, n, t* and suffixes *n, h* are permitted affixes.

   We minimise the error by matching the lexicon words that contain a CLS of length 3 or more, leaving out 126 (6%) short lexicon words.

3. **Scoring:** The CLS matching retrieves new words that are syntactically similar with the original words, therefore not all retrieved words are forms of these words; irrelevant words that have similar structure match as well: *hadame* (*humour*) matches with its form *mahdoum* (*humorous or cute*) and *tenhadam* (*get destroyed*). Such ambiguity exists because some letters represent two distinct Arabic phonemes, *d* for both ض and د in this case.

   FastText word embeddings projects word vectors based on their syntactic and semantic information (Bojanowski et al., 2017), we therefore utilise this feature to score all retrieved words based on their similarity with the original words. We give the original words a confidence score of 1, and sort all retrieved words from 1 (most relevant) to 0 (least relevant). We presume that the closer the retrieved words are to the original sentiment words the more likely they are to be forms of these words, as such we consider the similarity scores to be a measure of relatedness, consequently a measure of sentiment as well.

4. **Disambiguation:** Scoring the retrieved words made some automatic disambiguation possible. First, in case of a duplicate word or more per list, positive or negative, we keep the word with the highest score, since it resembles a high similarity with a lexicon word. Second, in case of words appearing in both the positive and negative lists, we also keep the ones with the higher scores in the list they pertain to: the positive *zalameh* (*bold man*) ambiguates with the negative *zalim* (*unjust*) because the letter *z* represents two distinct phonemes ز and ظ in Arabic. Both words share the same CLS (zlm), therefore the approach retrieves the same list of forms. After the disambiguation, the positive forms remain in the positive list and the negative forms in the negative list.

   The potential of this approach was apparent with many sentiment words reaching over 1K forms. We observed the retrieved words to find that most of them were inflectional and orthographic forms, except for some lexicon words that matched a high number of irrelevant forms: *wafa2* (*lucky* or *agree*) has a unique CLS of (wf2) matched 840 relevant forms, *3atel* (*useless*) on the other hand, shares a CLS (3tl) with a highly inflectional lexeme *b3atl* (*send to*), matched 1.36K words that are mostly irrelevant.

We acknowledge that perfecting the approach requires automatic filtering of the irrelevant matched words. We checked if the frequency of the matched words in the corpus or the number of words retrieved could serve as features to determine whether they are relevant to the original words, but unfortunately they do not. Both relevant and irrelevant words retrieved are syntactically similar, therefore filtering irrelevant words automatically might necessitates a measure of contextual similarity, which is what the more recent language models are capable of computing (Peters et al., 2018; Devlin et al., 2018; Radford et al., 2018). However, under the current circumstance of low-resource NLP, we were not able to train such models on the corpus at hand. Therefore, we added a manual filtering step.

5. **Filtering:** After expanding and disambiguating each word automatically, a Lebanese native post-graduate student checks whether the retrieved words, collectively[2], are mostly relevant or completely irrelevant to determine whether to expand the lexicon word. The student filtered out 103 (5%) lexicon words; although small in number, if each word expands to 1K, we harm the lexicon with 100K irrelevant words.

As a result, the proposed approach expanded 1.7K words to around 175K, a new morphologically and orthogaphic rich Lebanese Arabizi sentiment lexicon. We named it SenZi-Large and released it publicly on the project's page[3].

5 Evaluation

We now evaluate the proposed approach extrinsically by applying a lexicon-based sentiment classification against the small annotated dataset of 1.6K tweets mentioned in Section 4. We wish to have had a larger dataset to reveal the true coverage of SenZi-Large, nevertheless, we settle for showing the value of the lexical induction approach.

In the lexicon-based approach, we search every word from the annotated tweets across the sentiment lexicon to assign scores to the matched words. We set the associated score for words that match with the positive list, and set a negated associated score for words that match with the negative list. Finally, we sum the scores to classify the tweets as positive or negative.

Since this is a binary classification task, similar to Subtask B from SemEval-2017 Task 4 (Rosenthal et al., 2017), we present the percentage of the classified tweets and the classification results of these tweets separately in Table 1. We compare SenZi-Large (175K words) with the original lexicon (2K words) and the previous expansion SenZi (24.6K words) that is mentioned in Sections 2 and 4.

Table 1: Extrinsic Evaluation
Lexicon-Based Sentiment Classification
1.6K Tweets (800 positive, 800 negative)

Lexicon	Classified	R	P	F	A
Original	22%	0.94	0.87	0.90	0.90
SenZi	55%	0.94	0.77	0.85	0.82
SenZi-Large	68%	0.83	0.80	0.82	0.83

Recall, **P**recision, **F**1-Score (Macro-averaging), **A**ccuracy

Inducing morphological and orthographic forms for Arabizi using the proposed approach improved the lexicon coverage by a solid 13% over the previous expansion. The induction expanded 1.7K words to 175K, that is more than 100 new forms per lexicon word on average. Although we disambiguated the

[2]For efficiency, the student does not validate the retrieved words word by word, rather skims the whole list.

[3]`https://tahatobaili.github.io/project-rbz/`

retrieved words and filtered out some lexicon words, as expected, such a large induction introduced some noise, neutral or irrelevant words, that traded-off the the coverage gain for a 3% loss in the F1-Score over the previous version.

We now asses the classification errors to point out the limitations of the produced lexicon. Since the evaluation of the lexical induction was done on sentiment classification of Twitter data, we asses the error manually from Twitter words that were either unclassified or falsely classified.

We extract a sample of 100 tweets at random from the 1.6K tweets dataset, of which 58 were correctly classified, 12 falsely classified, and 30 unclassified. We balance the 12 falsely classified with 12 unclassified tweets at random for the error analysis. From these 24 tweets, we counted a vocabulary of 178 words[4] that contain 30 sentiment words. The approach missed 24 sentiment words and falsely classified 19 non-sentiment words. We present the distribution of error for each case below in Table 2.

Table 2: Error Analysis

Sample	Words	Error	Distribution
Unclassified Sentiment Words	24	Orthographic Variant	46%
		Code-switched	37%
		Other	17%
Falsely Classified Non-Sentiment Words	19	False Neighbour	42%
		Other	58%

Most of the sentiment words that were not covered by the lexicon are orthographic variants of words that do exist in the lexicon: SenZi contains *bitwatar, bietwatar, btwaterne, betwaterne...* forms of (*I get nervous*) but not *betawattar* that appeared in text. Codeswitching also appears to be an inevitable challenge in Lebanese Arabizi texting: *chu heydaa ktiir cute* (*whats that* (expression) *soo cute*). On the other hand, most of the falsely classified non-sentiment words are false neighbours that were retrieved in the induction: *m3alim* (*an expert*) matched with a false neighbour *ma3loumeh* (*piece of information*). The other types of unclassified or falsely classified words consist mainly of multi-word sentiment expressions and sarcasm or contextual and polysemic words, which are known challenges for the lexicon-based sentiment analysis in general (Liu, 2012).

6 Discussion

Spoken languages that lack a standard orthography tend to have a high degree of lexical sparsity, especially if they are morphologically rich as well. If words can be transcribed in a variety of ways without a consensus on an orthography, then they can not be referenced with one correct orthography. This by nature defies word classification tasks such as sentiment analysis, NER, POS tagging, word sense disambiguation (WSD), anaphora resolution, etc.

We proposed a new approach to match words with their inflectional and orthographic forms in a low-resourced context. We hand-crafted a rule based approach that worked well with the linguistic nitty gritty complexities of a highly-sparsed scripture, Arabizi, and coupled it with word embeddings using minimal resources. The limitation of this approach was adding a manual check to filter out the lexicon words that retrieved irrelevant words. In a resourceful situation however, we would have trained advanced word embedding models to measure the contextual similarity of the words, with the intention to automate this step. Such models require large amount of data to pre-train especially for uncommon languages like Arabizi. Nevertheless, the result was a new sentiment lexicon, SenZi-Large, composed of 175K forms induced from 1.7K words, 7 times larger than the previous expansion for a 3% trade-off in F1 score. We presented a word-level classification error analysis on the same Twitter data to learn that most of the missed words are either orthographic variants of SenZi's words or English sentiment words and most of the falsely classified words were false neighbours introduced in the large induction. This consolidates the significance of lexical sparsity in non-standard languages.

[4]Excluding short words that consist of one or two characters only and non-alphanumeric words.

Although the outcome is a new public resource, the main contribution of this work is the proposed approach. The essence of the approach is in normalising and connecting consonant letters which comprise the backbone of most Latin script vocabulary. In the case of Lebanese dialect Arabizi, we observed a set of prefixes and suffixes and used them to minimise the error in the induction. However, given the complexity of Arabic morphology described in Section 1, a rule-based approach is far from success. We therefore combined it with word embeddings to filter the irrelevant and score the sentiment words. As such, our intuition is that the approach could potentially be useful for at least other Arabizi dialects if not other Latin script languages that pose similar challenges, such as Javanese dialects and Alsatian (Millour and Fort, 2020). The approach might also be catered for other NLP tasks such as lemmatisation or text simplification in morphologically-rich languages.

7 Conclusion

In this work we addressed the issue of high-degree lexical sparsity for a social language under a severe circumstance of small resources that are considered insufficient to train recent powerful language models. We proposed a new rule-based approach that utilises classical word embeddings to connect words with their inflectional and orthographic forms from a given corpus. Our case example is the low-resourced Lebanese dialect Arabizi, hence we used and expanded the only available resources we found in the literature to test and evaluate the approach. We induced 175K forms from a list of 1.7K sentiment words. We evaluated this induction extrinsically on a sentiment-annotated dataset pushing its coverage by 13% over the previous version. We named the new lexicon SenZi-Large and released it publicly[5].

Latinising a non-Latin script language heuristically is not a novel phenomenon, as to Arabizi, Greek, Farsi, Hindi, Bengali, Urdu, Telugu, Tamil and other languages are also transcribed in Latin script, known as Greeklish (Androutsopoulos, 2012), Finglish, Hinglish (Sailaja, 2011), Binglish, etc. For a future work, we plan to explore cross-lingual approaches (Ruder et al., 2019) to bridge such low-resourced languages that are written in different scripts.

References

Mariam Aboelezz. 2009. Latinised arabic and connections to bilingual ability. In *Lancaster University Postgraduate Conference in Linguistics & Language Teaching. Lancaster, UK*, volume 3, pages 1–23.

Mohamed Al-Badrashiny, Ramy Eskander, Nizar Habash, and Owen Rambow. 2014. Automatic transliteration of romanized dialectal arabic. In *Proceedings of the Eighteenth Conference on Computational Natural Language Learning*, pages 30–38.

Jannis Androutsopoulos. 2012. Greeklish": Transliteration practice and discourse in the context of computer-mediated digraphia. *Orthography as social action: Scripts, spelling, identity and power*, pages 359–392.

Timothy Baldwin, Marie-Catherine de Marneffe, Bo Han, Young-Bum Kim, Alan Ritter, and Wei Xu. 2015. Shared tasks of the 2015 workshop on noisy user-generated text: Twitter lexical normalization and named entity recognition. In *Proceedings of the Workshop on Noisy User-generated Text*, pages 126–135.

Ramy Baly, Hazem Hajj, Nizar Habash, Khaled Bashir Shaban, and Wassim El-Hajj. 2017. A sentiment treebank and morphologically enriched recursive deep models for effective sentiment analysis in arabic. *ACM Transactions on Asian and Low-Resource Language Information Processing (TALLIP)*, 16(4):1–21.

Piotr Bojanowski, Edouard Grave, Armand Joulin, and Tomas Mikolov. 2017. Enriching word vectors with subword information. *Transactions of the Association for Computational Linguistics*, 5:135–146.

Danish Contractor, Tanveer A Faruquie, and L Venkata Subramaniam. 2010. Unsupervised cleansing of noisy text. In *Proceedings of the 23rd International Conference on Computational Linguistics: Posters*, pages 189–196. Association for Computational Linguistics.

Kareem Darwish. 2014. Arabizi detection and conversion to arabic. *ANLP 2014*, page 217.

[5]`https://tahatobaili.github.io/project-rbz/`

Leon Derczynski, Alan Ritter, Sam Clark, and Kalina Bontcheva. 2013. Twitter part-of-speech tagging for all: Overcoming sparse and noisy data. In *Proceedings of the International Conference Recent Advances in Natural Language Processing RANLP 2013*, pages 198–206.

Jacob Devlin, Ming-Wei Chang, Kenton Lee, and Kristina Toutanova. 2018. Bert: Pre-training of deep bidirectional transformers for language understanding. *arXiv preprint arXiv:1810.04805*.

Stephan Gouws, Dirk Hovy, and Donald Metzler. 2011. Unsupervised mining of lexical variants from noisy text. In *Proceedings of the First workshop on Unsupervised Learning in NLP*, pages 82–90. Association for Computational Linguistics.

Imane Guellil, Faiçal Azouaou, Mourad Abbas, and Sadat Fatiha. 2017. Arabizi transliteration of algerian arabic dialect into modern standard arabic. In *Social MT 2017/First workshop on Social Media and User Generated Content Machine Translation*.

Bo Han and Timothy Baldwin. 2011. Lexical normalisation of short text messages: Makn sens a# twitter. In *Proceedings of the 49th annual meeting of the association for computational linguistics: Human language technologies*, pages 368–378.

Bing Liu. 2012. Sentiment analysis and opinion mining. *Synthesis lectures on human language technologies*, 5(1):1–167.

Abir Masmoudi, Mariem Ellouze Khmekhem, Mourad Khrouf, and Lamia Hadrich Belguith. 2019. Transliteration of arabizi into arabic script for tunisian dialect. *ACM Transactions on Asian and Low-Resource Language Information Processing (TALLIP)*, 19(2):1–21.

Alice Millour and Karën Fort. 2020. Text corpora and the challenge of newly written languages. In *Proceedings of the 1st Joint Workshop on Spoken Language Technologies for Under-resourced languages (SLTU) and Collaboration and Computing for Under-Resourced Languages (CCURL)*, pages 111–120.

Sergiu Nisioi, Sanja Štajner, Simone Paolo Ponzetto, and Liviu P Dinu. 2017. Exploring neural text simplification models. In *Proceedings of the 55th Annual Meeting of the Association for Computational Linguistics (Volume 2: Short Papers)*, pages 85–91.

Matthew E Peters, Mark Neumann, Mohit Iyyer, Matt Gardner, Christopher Clark, Kenton Lee, and Luke Zettlemoyer. 2018. Deep contextualized word representations. *arXiv preprint arXiv:1802.05365*.

Alec Radford, Karthik Narasimhan, Tim Salimans, and Ilya Sutskever. 2018. Improving language understanding by generative pre-training.

Sara Rosenthal, Noura Farra, and Preslav Nakov. 2017. Semeval-2017 task 4: Sentiment analysis in twitter. In *Proceedings of the 11th international workshop on semantic evaluation (SemEval-2017)*, pages 502–518.

Sebastian Ruder, Ivan Vulić, and Anders Søgaard. 2019. A survey of cross-lingual word embedding models. *Journal of Artificial Intelligence Research*, 65:569–631.

Pingali Sailaja. 2011. Hinglish: code-switching in indian english. *ELT journal*, 65(4):473–480.

Djamé Seddah, Farah Essaidi, Amal Fethi, Matthieu Futeral, Benjamin Muller, Pedro Javier Ortiz Suárez, Benoît Sagot, and Abhishek Srivastava. 2020. Building a user-generated content north-african arabizi treebank: Tackling hell. In *Proceedings of the 58th Annual Meeting of the Association for Computational Linguistics*, pages 1139–1150.

Radu Soricut and Franz Josef Och. 2015. Unsupervised morphology induction using word embeddings. In *Proceedings of the 2015 Conference of the North American Chapter of the Association for Computational Linguistics: Human Language Technologies*, pages 1627–1637.

Natalie Sullivan. 2017. *Writing Arabizi: Orthographic Variation in Romanized Lebanese Arabic on Twitter*. Ph.D. thesis.

Taha Tobaili, Miriam Fernandez, Harith Alani, Sanaa Sharafeddine, Hazem Hajj, and Goran Glavaš. 2019. Senzi: A sentiment analysis lexicon for the latinised arabic (arabizi). In *Proceedings of the International Conference on Recent Advances in Natural Language Processing (RANLP 2019)*, pages 1203–1211.

Taha Tobaili. 2016. Arabizi identification in twitter data. In *Proceedings of the ACL 2016 Student Research Workshop*, pages 51–57.

Mohammad Ali Yaghan. 2008. "arabizi": A contemporary style of arabic slang. *Design issues*, 24(2):39–52.

NILC at SR'20: Exploring Pre-Trained Models in Surface Realisation

Marco Antonio Sobrevilla Cabezudo msobrevillac@usp.br

Thiago Alexandre Salgueiro Pardo taspardo@icmc.usp.br

Núcleo Interinstitucional de Linguística Computacional (NILC)
Instituto de Ciências Matemáticas e de Computação, Universidade de São Paulo
Avenida Trabalhador São-carlense, 400. São Carlos - SP - Brazil

Abstract

This paper describes the submission by the NILC Computational Linguistics research group of the University of São Paulo/Brazil to the English Track 2 (closed sub-track) at the Surface Realisation Shared Task 2020. The success of the current pre-trained models like BERT or GPT-2 in several tasks is well-known, however, this is not the case for data-to-text generation tasks and just recently some initiatives focused on it. This way, we explore how a pre-trained model (GPT-2) performs on the UD-to-text generation task. In general, the achieved results were poor, but there are some interesting ideas to explore. Among the learned lessons we may note that it is necessary to study strategies to represent UD inputs and to introduce structural knowledge into these pre-trained models.

1 Introduction

Universal Dependencies[1] (UD) have gained relevance in the Natural Language Processing (NLP) community. UD treebanks have already proved useful in the development of multilingual applications, becoming an advantage for developers.

One of the successful applications of UD is related to Data-to-text generation. This may be seen in the two shared-tasks proposed (Mille et al., 2018; Mille et al., 2019) in which there were several participants. In general, the Surface Realisation Shared Task aims to continue with the development of natural language generation methods focused on the surface realisation task. Specifically, models in this task must generate sentences from dependency trees (or similar structures) in CoNLL format.

This task comprises two tracks: (1) the Shallow Track, in which word order and word forms are removed from the UD structure, and (2) the Deep Track, which, in addition to the word order and word forms, functional words, morphological features and other kinds of information are removed or changed in the UD structure to make it more similar to a semantic representation (called deep syntax).

Diverse approaches have been applied on this shared task in previous editions, being mainly divided in inflection generation and word ordering tasks (Mille et al., 2019). Besides, there is a trend to use neural models for the same tasks.

Recently, pre-trained language models have become standard in a variety of Natural Language Processing (NLP) tasks (Peters et al., 2018; Devlin et al., 2019; Radford et al., 2019), including sentence-level classification, sequence tagging and question answering. These models can be pre-trained on large corpora of available unannotated text, and then fine-tuned for specific tasks on smaller amounts of supervised data, relying on the induced language model structure to facilitate generalisation beyond the annotations.

These pre-trained models have been widely used in text-to-text generation tasks such as text simplification, automatic summarisation, and machine translation, obtaining good results and outperforming the current state of the art. However, there are few initiatives for the data-to-text generation task. Lately, Mager et al. (2020) used GPT-2 for fine-tuning AMR-to-text generation task, showing improvements and

[1]Available at https://universaldependencies.org/

Proceedings of the Third Workshop on Multilingual Surface Realisation (MSR'20), pages 50–56
Barcelona, Spain (Online), December 12, 2020.

that current pre-trained models can handle these representations even if the knowledge is not explicitly structured.

In this context, this paper presents the description of the system submitted by the NILC team to the track 2 of the Surface Realisation Shared Task 2020 (Track 2 - SR'20) (Mille et al., 2020). Our proposal is an End-to-End approach inspired by the work of Mager et al. (2020). We explore some strategies to sequentially represent UD structures and to fine-tune GPT-2 (Radford et al., 2019) on the pre-processed dataset[2].

2 Track 2 Dataset - SR'20

The dataset for the Track 2 is composed by UD structures and their corresponding sentences. The UD structure is similar to a dependency tree, however, some information are modified:

- word order is removed by randomised scrambling;
- words are replaced by their lemmas;
- some prepositions and conjunctions (that can be inferred from other lexical units or from the syntactic structure) are removed;
- determiners and auxiliaries are replaced (when needed) by attribute/value pairs;
- edge labels were generalised into predicate argument labels in the PropBank/NomBank fashion;
- morphological information coming from the syntactic structure or from agreement is removed;
- only coarse-grained Part-of-Speech tags are kept.

Figure 1 and 2 show the CoNLL and graphic representation for the sentence "Two of them were being run by 2 officials of the Ministry of the Interior!". In Figure 1, we may see "*idX*" and "*original_id*" attributes, where "X" can be a number. This attributes are related to the track 1 and the original ids (positions) of the tokens in the sentence and are removed from the test set.

```
run     _     VERB    _     Tense=Pres|id2=8|id1=12|id3=13|original_id=6|Aspect=Prog|ClauseType=Exc 0   ROOT  _  _
official      _       NOUN  _     Number=Plur|id2=3|id1=16|original_id=9  1   AM  _  _
two     _     NUM  _  NumType=Card|id1=6|original_id=1    1   A2  _  _
Ministry      _       PROPN _     Number=Sing|id2=14|id1=11|id3=15|original_id=12|Definite=Def    2   AM  _  _
2       _     NUM  _  NumType=Card|id1=10|original_id=8   2   A1INV   _  _
they    _     PRON    _     Number=Plur|id2=2|id1=4|original_id=3|Person=3|PronType=Prs 3   AM  _  _
Interior      _       PROPN _     Number=Sing|id2=7|id1=5|id3=9|original_id=15|Definite=Def   4   AM  _  _
```

Figure 1: Deep track example ("Two of them were being run by 2 officials of the Ministry of the Interior!") in CoNLL format.

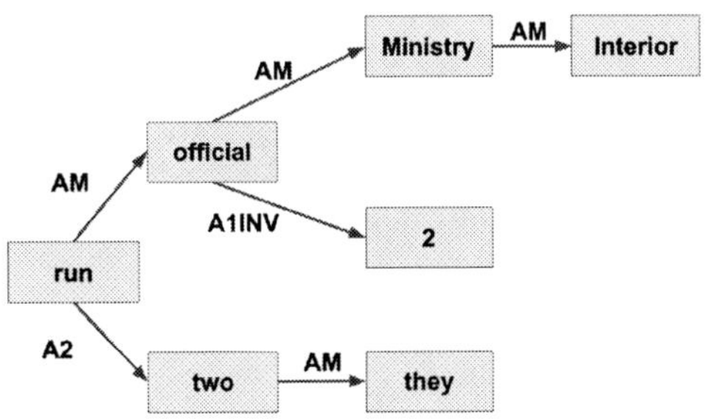

Figure 2: Representation of the example in graphic format.

[2]The corresponding source code is available at `https://github.com/msobrevillac/pretrained-amr-to-text`

Finally, the dataset contains subsets from different domains. For English (our target language in this task), there are 4 files in the training and development (dev) set each, and 7 files for the test set from the previous edition (Mille et al., 2019) and 1 file for the test set in this edition.

3 System Description

In first edition of this shared task, we submit a system in which we use a data augmentation strategy (Sobrevilla Cabezudo and Pardo, 2018) to deal with the track 1. However, for this edition, we focus on the track 2 and use only resources allowed by the shared task (closed sub-track). Differently from most of the work found in the literature, we propose an End-to-End approach, jointly learning the inflection generation and word ordering tasks.

3.1 GPT-2 for UD structures

Inspired by the work of Mager et al. (2020), we use GPT-2 and fine-tune on the joint distribution of UD structure and text. Given a tokenized sentence $w_1 w_N$ and the sequential UD structure $a_1...a_M$, we maximize the joint probability.

$$p_{GPT-2}(w,a) = \prod_{j=1}^{N} p_{GPT-2}(w_j|w_{1:j-1}, u_{1:M}) \prod_{i=1}^{M} p_{GPT-2}(u_i|u_{1:i-1}) \tag{1}$$

A special separator token is added to mark the end of the sequential UD structure. Relations that should not be interpreted literally are assigned tokens from the GPT-2 unused token list (adding a ":" to mark the token as a relation). Furthermore, in the case of morphological information, values in feature name-value pairs are considered common tokens and feature names are considered relations. For example, in Figure 1, the token "run" has "Tense=Pres" as a feature name-value pair. This way, "Pres" is considered a common token and "Tense" a relation. At test time, we provide the UD structure as context as in conventional conditional text generation.

It is worth noting that we explore different ways to build the sequential (linearised) UD structure, and all these sequential versions are derived from the PENMAN notation. We explore the following linearised versions:

(A) PENMAN format: this format is the same one used in Abstract Meaning Representation (AMR);

(B) PENMAN format without morphological relations: the same format, but removing all morphological relations (and others in the same column), such as "Tense" and "Aspect", among others;

(C) PENMAN format without morphological relations and parentheses;

(D) PENMAN format without parentheses: the same as the first one but removing the parentheses;

(E) PENMAN format without relations: the same as the first one but removing all the relations;

(F) PENMAN format without relations and parentheses: the same as the first one but removing all the relations and parentheses.

Figure 3 shows three representations for the example in Figure 1: (A) PENMAN notation, (B) PENMAN notation without morphological relations, and (C) PENMAN notation without morphological relations and parentheses. It is interesting to add that the parentheses in PENMAN notation provide information about the graph structure of the input.

```
(A)  ( run :tense pres :aspect prog :clausetype exc
         :am ( official :number plur
              :am ( Ministry :number sing :definite def
                   :am ( Interior :number sing :definite def ) )
              :a1inv ( 2 :numtype card ) )
         :a2 ( two :numtype card
              :am ( they :number plur :person 3 :prontype prs ) ) )

(B)  ( run pres prog exc
         :am ( official plur
              :am ( Ministry sing def
                   :am ( Interior sing def ) )
                   :a1inv ( 2 card ) )
         :a2 ( two card
              :am ( they plur 3 prs ) ) )

(C)  run pres prog exc :am official plur :am Ministry sing def :am Interior sing def :a1inv 2 card
     :a2 two card :am they plur 3 prs
```

Figure 3: Sequential UD structures for the sentence "Two of them were being run by 2 officials of the Ministry of the Interior!". (A) PENMAN notation, (B) PENMAN notation without morphological relations, and (C) PENMAN notation without morphological relations and parentheses.

3.2 Settings

We use the small GPT-2 model provided by HuggingFace (Wolf et al., 2019)[3]. The model is trained on the joint of all training subsets. The fine-tuning is executed in 7 epochs (as the model converges at this time), using a batch size of 8, the AdamW optimizer with a learning rate of 6.25e-5, a max length of 350 in the source and target, and freezing the embeddings. For the decoding, we use a beam size of 15.

At test time, we get tokenised sentences. We then post-process them by using the Moses detokeniser[4].

4 Results and Discussion

The automatic performance of the diverse proposals at the shared task is computed by the following measures:

- BLEU (Papineni et al., 2002): precision metric that computes the geometric mean of the n-gram precisions between the generated and reference texts, adding a brevity penalty for shorter sentences (we use the smoothed version and report results for n = 1, 2, 3, and 4);
- NIST (Doddington, 2002): related n-gram similarity metric weighted in favor of less frequent n-grams, which are taken to be more informative;
- Normalized edit distance (DIST): inverse, normalized, character-based string-edit distance that starts by computing the minimum number of character insertions, deletions and substitutions (all at cost 1) required to turn the system output into the (single) reference text;
- BertScore (Zhang et al., 2020): leverages the pre-trained contextual embeddings from BERT and matches words in candidate and reference sentences by cosine similarity.

Table 1 shows the results of the different linearised versions (described in Section 3.1 of the UD structures on the development set). The results are the ones obtained on the join of all dev subsets provided by the shared-task.

In general, morphological relations do not seem to be necessary as the performance improves when these are removed (B in Table 1). However, a possible noise in this analysis could be generated by

[3] We use only the small GPT-2 version as we could not execute this on our current server.

[4] We use the perl code available at https://github.com/moses-smt/mosesdecoder/tree/master/scripts/tokenizer

the input length since including morphological relations (linearised version A in Table 1) could make the input length larger and the max length parameter could delete some important tokens, resulting in a lower performance in comparison with linearised version B.

To make the analysis of omitting morphological relations clearer, we may see versions C (without parentheses and morphological relations) and D (without parentheses). Both versions contain fewer tokens (in relation to A and B versions) and one may see that disregarding morphological relations produces improvements (results in version C are better than in D).

Another point to note is that parentheses are the most important tokens as they represent the structure of the input. Therefore, removing them from the input leads to a significant drop in the performance (D). Furthermore, this drop is bigger than the one obtained by leaving out all the relations (E), showing that parentheses could encode some information about the relations among the nodes. Finally, the results of the F version could suggest that, although parentheses encode some information about the relations, there are more information that is not encoded, making the use of relations (in general) necessary.

Linearised version	BLEU	NIST	BertScore
(A)	39.28	9.65	0.9390
(B)	42.52	10.29	0.9413
(C)	36.67	9.82	0.9350
(D)	35.89	9.59	0.9347
(E)	38.00	9.97	0.9354
(F)	27.61	8.83	0.9228

Table 1: Results with different inputs on the dev set.

Table 2 shows the results of the automatic evaluation on several test sets. The model that we use to get these results is the one that got the best results in the dev set. In general, Table 2 shows that all values are close to the average (except for the test set presented in this edition). This could suggest that GPT-2 can keep a similar performance across the domains, i.e., it can generalise well. Finally, our approach got a performance lower than other approaches for the same track. However, we expect that these differences could be reduced if we use a bigger model such as medium or large GPT-2 (similar to the results of Mager et al. (2020)).

Table 3 shows the results of the human evaluation on two test sets predefined by the organizing committee. Specifically, Direct Assessment (Graham et al., 2017) is applied to conduct this evaluation. Candidate outputs are presented to human assessors, who rate their (i) meaning similarity (relative to a human-authored reference sentence) and (ii) readability (no reference sentence) on a 0-100 rating scale. The metric used for ranking the different systems is the average standardised score (avg. z in Table 3. We may see that our approach still have problems representing the correct reference as this gets the worst performance according to the meaning similarity (last cluster). However, when readability is evaluated,

		BLEU	NIST	DIST	BertScore
2020	en_filtered_lines-fix	39.68	9.31	57.56	0.9317
	en_pud	42.60	9.68	59.85	0.9382
	en_ewt-Pred-HIT-edit	43.15	9.64	62.20	0.9392
	en_pud-Pred-LATTICE	42.64	9.59	60.43	0.9368
2019	en_ewt	45.19	9.96	64.83	0.9411
	en_gum	40.94	9.00	60.42	0.9399
	en_lines	41.04	9.09	61.18	0.9381
	en_partut	43.41	8.24	59.74	0.9438
Average		42.33	9.31	60.78	0.9386

Table 2: Results of our system on the test set.

Meaning Similarity							Readability						
Test set	Team	Sub-track	Avg.	Avg. z	n	N	Test set	Team	Sub-track	Avg.	Avg. z	n	N
English (EWT)	IMS	20b	85.1	0.272	1,667	1,927	English (EWT)	Concordia	20a	71.8	0.321	806	908
	IMS	20a	84.7	0.259	1,701	1,942		Ours	20a	68.6	0.185	823	947
	Concordia	20a	84.7	0.245	1,675	1,897		IMS	20b	67.3	0.159	807	936
	IMS	19	82.7	0.201	1,692	1,920		IMS	20a	65.8	0.109	753	866
	Ours	20a	75.6	-0.079	1,657	1,892		IMS	19	63.6	0.027	808	923
English (Wiki)	IMS	20b	87.3	0.157	700	1,016	English (Wiki)	Concordia	20a	80.6	0.37	952	1,283
	IMS	20a	85.6	0.057	755	1,078		Ours	20a	75.4	0.213	930	1,273
	IMS	19	85.5	0.025	698	1,023		IMS	20b	70.2	0.055	932	1,256
	Concordia	20a	84.7	-0.029	715	1,036		IMS	20a	69	-0.03	963	1,284
	RALI	19	76	-0.463	720	1,044		IMS	19	67.3	-0.095	932	1,233
	Ours	20a	76.6	-0.491	721	1,088		RALI	19	56.1	-0.562	940	1,329

Table 3: Results of the human evaluation for the track 2. Meaning Similarity and Readability are computed. Avg. is the average 0-100% received by systems. Avg. z is the corresponding average standardised scores. "n" is the total number of distinct test sentences assessed, and N is the total number of human judgments. The results are sorted by avg. z. and horizontal lines indicate clusters, such that systems in a cluster all significantly outperform all the systems in lower ranked clusters.

we obtain the second best results (second cluster), even compared with approaches in the open subtrack (20b) in which all kinds of resources are allowed.

These results are expected as the automatic evaluation shows a low performance for our approach and it is reflected in the meaning similarity evaluation, while GPT-2 is a robust language model and knows how to build coherent sentences (we have to stress that readability is evaluated without references). More experiments could be done in order to explore how to get improvements in meaning similarity. Experiments performed by Mager et al. (2020) show that the performance improves significantly when a bigger version of GPT-2 is used. Besides, we may see that the performance varies widely according to the linearisation strategy, which would be an interesting research line to explore in the future.

5 Conclusion and Future Work

This paper describes the application of a pre-trained model, the GPT-2, to the UD-to-text generation task in the context of the Surface Realisation shared task. Results show that the way as the UD structures are linearised is important for the model in this task. Thus, an interesting research line for future work could be investigating other ways to represent/linearise UD structures and to introduce the knowledge about structure in this kind of model. As future work, we also plan to apply this approach to other languages and use a bigger version of GPT-2.

Acknowledgements

This work was financed in part by the *Coordenação de Aperfeiçoamento de Pessoal de Nível Superior – Brasil (CAPES)* – Finance Code 88882.328822/2019-01. The authors are also grateful to USP Research Office (PRP 668) for supporting this work, and would like to thank NVIDIA for donating the GPU. This work is part of the OPINANDO project (`https://sites.google.com/icmc.usp.br/opinando/`) and the USP/FAPESP/IBM Center for Artificial Intelligence (C4AI - `http://c4ai.inova.usp.br/`). Finally, this research is carried out using the computational resources of the Center for Mathematical Sciences Applied to Industry (CeMEAI) funded by FAPESP (grant 2013/07375-0).

References

Jacob Devlin, Ming-Wei Chang, Kenton Lee, and Kristina Toutanova. 2019. BERT: Pre-training of deep bidirectional transformers for language understanding. In *Proceedings of the 2019 Conference of the North American Chapter of the Association for Computational Linguistics: Human Language Technologies, Volume 1 (Long and Short Papers)*, pages 4171–4186, Minneapolis, Minnesota, June. Association for Computational Linguistics.

George Doddington. 2002. Automatic evaluation of machine translation quality using n-gram co-occurrence statistics. In *Proceedings of the Second International Conference on Human Language Technology Research*, HLT '02, pages 138–145, San Francisco, CA, USA. Morgan Kaufmann Publishers Inc.

Yvette Graham, Timothy Baldwin, Alistair Moffat, and Justin Zobel. 2017. Can machine translation systems be evaluated by the crowd alone. *Natural Language Engineering*, 23(1):3–30.

Manuel Mager, Ramón Fernandez Astudillo, Tahira Naseem, Md Arafat Sultan, Young-Suk Lee, Radu Florian, and Salim Roukos. 2020. GPT-too: A language-model-first approach for AMR-to-text generation. In *Proceedings of the 58th Annual Meeting of the Association for Computational Linguistics*, pages 1846–1852, Online, July. Association for Computational Linguistics.

Simon Mille, Anja Belz, Bernd Bohnet, Yvette Graham, Emily Pitler, and Leo Wanner. 2018. The first multilingual surface realisation shared task (SR'18): Overview and evaluation results. In *Proceedings of the First Workshop on Multilingual Surface Realisation*, pages 1–12, Melbourne, Australia, July. Association for Computational Linguistics.

Simon Mille, Anja Belz, Bernd Bohnet, Yvette Graham, and Leo Wanner. 2019. The second multilingual surface realisation shared task (SR'19): Overview and evaluation results. In *Proceedings of the 2nd Workshop on Multilingual Surface Realisation (MSR 2019)*, pages 1–17, Hong Kong, China, November. Association for Computational Linguistics.

Simon Mille, Anya Belz, Bernd Bohnet, Thiago Castro Ferreira, Yvette Graham, and Leo Wanner. 2020. The third multilingual surface realisation shared task (SR'20): Overview and evaluation results. In *Proceedings of the 3nd Workshop on Multilingual Surface Realisation (MSR 2020)*, Dublin, Ireland, December. Association for Computational Linguistics.

Kishore Papineni, Salim Roukos, Todd Ward, and Wei-Jing Zhu. 2002. Bleu: a method for automatic evaluation of machine translation. In *Proceedings of the 40th Annual Meeting of the Association for Computational Linguistics*, pages 311–318, Philadelphia, Pennsylvania, USA. Association for Computational Linguistics.

Matthew Peters, Mark Neumann, Mohit Iyyer, Matt Gardner, Christopher Clark, Kenton Lee, and Luke Zettlemoyer. 2018. Deep contextualized word representations. In *Proceedings of the 2018 Conference of the North American Chapter of the Association for Computational Linguistics: Human Language Technologies, Volume 1 (Long Papers)*, pages 2227–2237, New Orleans, Louisiana, June. Association for Computational Linguistics.

Alec Radford, Jeff Wu, Rewon Child, David Luan, Dario Amodei, and Ilya Sutskever. 2019. Language models are unsupervised multitask learners.

Marco Antonio Sobrevilla Cabezudo and Thiago Pardo. 2018. NILC-SWORNEMO at the surface realization shared task: Exploring syntax-based word ordering using neural models. In *Proceedings of the First Workshop on Multilingual Surface Realisation*, pages 58–64, Melbourne, Australia, July. Association for Computational Linguistics.

Thomas Wolf, Lysandre Debut, Victor Sanh, Julien Chaumond, Clement Delangue, Anthony Moi, Pierric Cistac, Tim Rault, R'emi Louf, Morgan Funtowicz, and Jamie Brew. 2019. Huggingface's transformers: State-of-the-art natural language processing. *ArXiv*, abs/1910.03771.

Tianyi Zhang, Varsha Kishore*, Felix Wu*, Kilian Q. Weinberger, and Yoav Artzi. 2020. Bertscore: Evaluating text generation with bert. In *International Conference on Learning Representations*.

Surface Realization Using Pretrained Language Models

Farhood Farahnak and **Laya Rafiee** and **Leila Kosseim** and **Thomas Fevens**
Concordia University
Montreal, Canada
firstname.lastname@concordia.ca

Abstract

In the context of Natural Language Generation, surface realization is the task of generating the linear form of a text following a given grammar. Surface realization models usually consist of a cascade of complex sub-modules, either rule-based or neural network-based, each responsible for a specific sub-task. In this work, we show that a single encoder-decoder language model can be used in an end-to-end fashion for all sub-tasks of surface realization. The model is designed based on the BART language model that receives a linear representation of unordered and non-inflected tokens in a sentence along with their corresponding Universal Dependency information and produces the linear sequence of inflected tokens along with the missing words. The model was evaluated on the shallow and deep tracks of the 2020 Surface Realization Shared Task (SR'20) using both human and automatic evaluation. The results indicate that despite its simplicity, our model achieves competitive results among all participants in the shared task.

1 Introduction

Natural Language Generation (NLG) models aim to generate fluent human-like texts given structured data. This involves both *content planning* (selecting the content to communicate) and *surface realization* (selecting, ordering, and inflecting the actual words) (Hovy et al., 1997; Reiter and Dale, 2000). This paper focuses on the second sub-task: Surface Realization (SR).

Unlike many tasks in Natural Language Processing (NLP), the performance of SR models are still below human performance. In order to fill this gap and encourage more research in this field, several shared tasks in NLG and SR have been proposed. In particular, since 2018, the Surface Realization Shared Tasks (Mille et al., 2018; Mille et al., 2019; Mille et al., 2020) were introduced to provide common-ground datasets for developing and evaluating NLG systems. This year, the task (Mille et al., 2020) proposed two tracks in several languages including English: 1) Track1: *shallow track* and 2) Track2: *deep track*. In the shallow track, unordered and lemmatized tokens with Universal Dependency (UD) structures (de Marneffe et al., 2014) were provided to participants and systems were required to reorder and inflect the tokens to produce final sentences. The deep track was similar to the shallow track but functional words and surface-oriented morphological information were not provided and had to be inferred by the systems. Therefor, in addition to determining the order and the inflection of tokens, systems participating in the deep track had to guess the omitted words.

Considering that the input data is in the form of Universal Dependency (UD) structure, data-to-text models, and graph-to-text models in particular, seem to be the right choice for the task of surface realization. However, in this study, we take a different path to tackle the problem. Our proposed model is designed based on text-to-text approaches using a pretrained encoder-decoder language model. More specifically, a BART (Lewis et al., 2020) language model is used for the task of surface realization for both the shallow and the deep tracks. The proposed approach is an end-to-end model trained on a linearized representation of the graph of the sentences with their corresponding Universal Dependency

Proceedings of the Third Workshop on Multilingual Surface Realisation (MSR'20), pages 57–63
Barcelona, Spain (Online), December 12, 2020.

information. The results on the English datasets demonstrate the potential of these models for surface realization tasks and in general data-to-text problems.

In the following sections, we first review recent and related approaches in surface realization and text-to-text models, then in Section 3, our proposed model is explained. Section 4 describes the results of our model on the surface realization datasets. Finally, Section 5 discusses conclusion and future work.

2 Related Work

Surface realization typically involves three tasks: syntactic realization, morphological realization, and orthographic realization (Reiter and Dale, 2000). Syntactic realization tries to identify the proper ordering of the input data, whereas morphological and orthographic realization are responsible for word inflections, punctuation, and formatting.

Several surface realization models presented at the previous Surface Realization Shared Task (Mille et al., 2019) used a cascade of pointer-based models for syntactic realization followed by another neural network module for morphological and orthographic realization (Du and Black, 2019; Farahnak et al., 2019; Mazzei and Basile, 2019). For example, Du *et al.* (2019) utilized a graph attention network (GAT) (Veličković et al., 2018) for encoding the input sentences and a pointer decoder (Vinyals et al., 2015) to select the next element from their graph. Whereas Yu *et al.* (2019) used a bidirectional Tree-LSTM (Zhou et al., 2016) as the encoder and an LSTM (Hochreiter and Schmidhuber, 1997) as the decoder and multiple LSTM modules for morphological and orthographic realization tasks. These two approaches achieved the highest performance among all participating systems at SR'19.

On the other hand, when the text to generate is conditioned on the content provided in the form of graphs, tables, etc then data-to-text generation models are utilized. As a family of data-to-text models, graph-to-text generation tries to generate natural text given its input graph. Graph-to-text generation models employ graph encoders to obtain a suitable representation from the input graph. Several applications such as text summarization (Duan et al., 2017), question answering (Fan et al., 2019), as well as surface realization (Du and Black, 2019) have used these types of generation models.

Recently, several works have proposed to use language models in the form of text-to-text for what is inherently data-to-text and particularly graph-to-text tasks (Kale, 2020; Mager et al., 2020; Harkous et al., 2020). Instead of modeling the node and edges of the graphs, they mapped the graph structure as sequences of words and let the language model encode the graph information. Kale (2020) takes advantage of T5 (Raffel et al., 2019) for data-to-text problems, whereas Mager *et al.* (2020) and Harkous *et al.* (2020) utilize GPT2 (Radford et al., 2019).

Following this recent trend of text-to-text models for graph-based problems, we developed an end-to-end approach based on a language model for the problem of data-to-text generation. The approach maps the given Universal Dependency structures to surface forms to tackle all the tasks required for the surface realization.

3 Model

Following the success of pretrained language models for data-to-text generation (Kale, 2020; Harkous et al., 2020), we tackled the surface realization problem using a similar approach. BART (Lewis et al., 2020) is an encoder-decoder language model based on transformers (Vaswani et al., 2017). Specifically, BART is a denoising autoencoder model trained on several denoising tasks making it applicable for a variety of downstream NLP tasks. The language model is trained to first encode the input, and then generate the text based on its input representation. The encoder-decoder architecture of BART makes it suitable for our task where the encoder module encodes the graph representation into an embedding space then the decoder generates the inflected form of the input one token at each decoding step. Hence, the model performs syntactic, morphological, and orthographic realization all at the same time.

In order to take advantage of a pretrained language model, BART in our case, we first need to map the graph structure of the input into a linear representation (i.e. plain text). For this task, given all the Universal Dependency (UD) information provided by the SR'20 organizers, we considered using only `LEMMA`, `UPOS`, `FEATS`, `HEAD`, and `DEPREL` for each node. Figure 1 shows the mapping structure with

```
     ...
(a)  26    kill    killed  VERB    VBD    Mood=Ind|Tense=Past|VerbForm=Fin|original_id=7  20    parataxis    _    _
     ...
(b)                    <s> LEMMA < HEAD > UPOS | FEATS | DEPREL <\s>

(c)                ... <s> kill < Al > VERB | Ind Past Fin | parataxis <\s> ...
```

Figure 1: A sample token with its linearized representation. The sample token with index 26 and its Universal Dependency (UD) information in (a) will be encoded using (b) to generate its linearized representation in (c).

an example of a linearized node. As Figure 1 shows, we concatenate each token with its corresponding features where special tokens <, >, | identify the boundary of each feature and special tokens such as the beginning of sentence <s> and end of sentence <\s> determine the boundary of each node (i.e. token). In these mapped representations, instead of the index for the `HEAD` feature, the actual token of the `HEAD` is used.

As opposed to previous work where tokens are selected among the input (Du and Black, 2019; Mazzei and Basile, 2019), the BART decoder generates tokens at each decoding step. As a result, we have no control on the number of tokens that should be generated. This can lead the model to generate extra tokens or ignore some of the input tokens. To alleviate this issue, we considered the tokenized form of the target sentences as the targets of the model. This allows the model to learn to map each node representation in its input into a token in the output and achieve a 1:1 mapping between the number of nodes in the input and the number of output tokens. An alternative would be to train on the detokenized output form but for the sake of automatic evaluation of the shared task, we did not follow this option.

4 Experiments and Results

4.1 Datasets

The proposed text-to-text surface realizer model was evaluated on the English datasets of the SR'20 (Mille et al., 2020). The datasets were created using the Universal Dependency (UD) datasets (de Marneffe et al., 2014) where the tokens within each sentence were randomly shuffled and the inflections were removed. The training and development sets were accompanied by 7 features. Out of these, the `FEATS` feature contained the relative linear order with respect to the governor (`Lin`) in addition to more than 40 morphological sub-features from the universal feature inventory. Among the four English datasets provided for training, we only trained on `en_ewt-ud-train` while the performance of the model was measured on all the eight test sets provided by the organizers (see Table 1).

4.2 Model Configuration

We used the pretrained BART-large model provided in the Huggingface library (Wolf et al., 2019). This model has 12 layers in each encoder and decoder modules. For each task, we trained our models with the same cross-entropy loss function as suggested in the original paper of BART and AdamW algorithm (Loshchilov and Hutter, 2019) with batch size of 2 and the learning rate of $1e-5$ for 20 epochs where these hyper-parameters are chosen based on the development set. For efficiency in training time, sentences longer than 35 tokens were removed from the training set. During inference, we used beam search with a size of 5.

4.3 Results

Our surface realization model was evaluated on all seven test sets from SR'19 and one new test set (`en_Wikipedia`) for SR'20. Results with all test sets are presented in Table 1 where *in-domain* refers to set-ups where test sets and training sets are from the same domain, while *out-of-domain* refers to set-ups where test sets are not in the same domain as the training sets. Two types of test sets were provided: *ud* and *pred*. The *ud* test sets contain the original UD datasets; whereas the *pred* test sets contain automatic predicted parse trees. Since we only trained our model on `en_ewt-ud-train`, all the other test sets should be considered out-of-domain for our model.

#		Dataset	T1 BLEU	T1 NIST	T1 DIST	T1 BERTScore	T2 BLEU	T2 NIST	T2 DIST	T2 BERTScore
1	In-domain	`en_ewt-ud`	70.71	12.70	77.94	0.9565	58.44	11.61	73.66	0.9635
2		`en_ewt-Pred`	67.12	12.40	74.47	0.9562	56.01	11.19	69.00	0.9593
3	Out-of-domain	`en_pud-ud`	74.47	12.62	76.46	0.9605	**58.45**	11.43	68.83	**0.9613**
4		`en_pud-Pred`	73.41	12.52	77.68	0.9596	**56.69**	11.18	67.79	**0.9584**
5		`en_gum-ud`	66.98	11.62	69.87	0.9555	53.92	10.51	67.02	0.9572
6		`en_lines-ud`	62.70	11.30	68.62	0.9565	47.96	9.93	64.33	0.9487
7		`en_partut-ud`	67.05	9.83	71.59	0.9565	**50.54**	8.57	62.39	0.9505
8		`en_Wikipedia`	74.66	12.90	76.93	0.9614	**57.49**	11.57	67.26	0.9473

Table 1: Results of our submission in the shallow (T1) and deep (T2) tracks of SR'20. Highlighted values indicate the highest score among all participants achieved by our model.

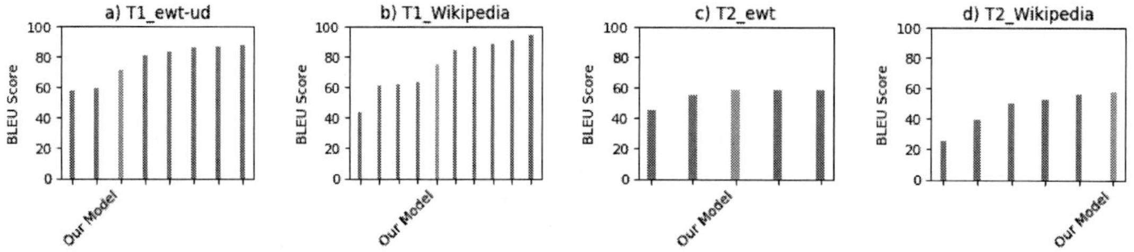

Figure 2: Comparison of all systems submitted to SR'20 on the `en_ewt-ud` and `en_Wikipedia` test sets for the shallow (T1) and the deep (T2) tracks evaluated based on their BLEU score.

Our models were evaluated both with automatic metrics and human evaluation. For the automatic metrics, as shown in Table 1, each test set was evaluated using four different metrics: BLEU, NIST, DIST, and BERTScore.

Figure 2 compares the BLEU score of our model with all other participants with the test sets `en_ewt-ud` and `en_Wikipedia` for both shallow (T1) and deep (T2) tracks. As Figure 2 shows, our model's performance falls close to the median of the other models in the shared task for the shallow track. However, in the deep track, our model performs best (Figure 2d) or close to the best (Figure 2c). These results seem to indicate that BART can better predict functional words and surface-oriented morphological information (required only in deep track) and this is mainly due to the denoising approaches used for training BART.

For human evaluation, SR'20 used Direct Assessment (Graham et al., 2017) where human assessors rated the output of systems based on meaning similarity (relative to a human-authored reference sentence) and readability (without reference sentences). Figure 3 shows the average score for the meaning similarity and readability on both shallow and deep tracks on two test sets: `en_ewt-ud` nad `en_Wikipedia`. In terms of readability, in the deep track, our model achieved the highest score after Human (see Figure 3a). However, in the shallow track, our performance is at the median of all participants. On the other hand, the meaning similarity of our model is lower than the best performing model (see Figure 3b). These comparisons indicate that although our model is able to generate well-written texts, their meaning are not close enough to the target sentences.

In order to have a better understanding of the model's behaviour, we further analyzed the generated outputs of our model. Our decoder generates tokens from its encoder hidden space, which is in contrast with ordering models where the output is selected from their input. This characteristic can have two impacts: A) the model does not restrict the output to the words in the input and it has no control over the number tokens it should generate. As a result, the model can generate extra tokens or ignore tokens from the input. Example A in Table 2 highlights this issue where the model did not generate the token *Ali*. B) the model generates long tokens in more than a single decoding step which makes it too complex for the model to have control over the details of such tokens. This behaviour is shown in Table 2 Example B. In this example, even though the model was able to generate a very complex URL similar to its input, there

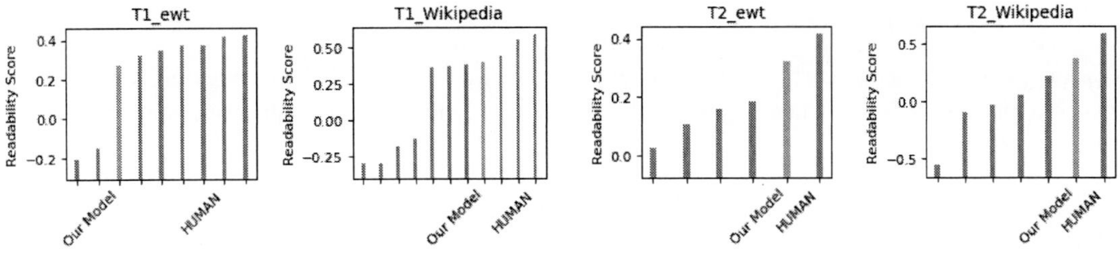

(a) Readability

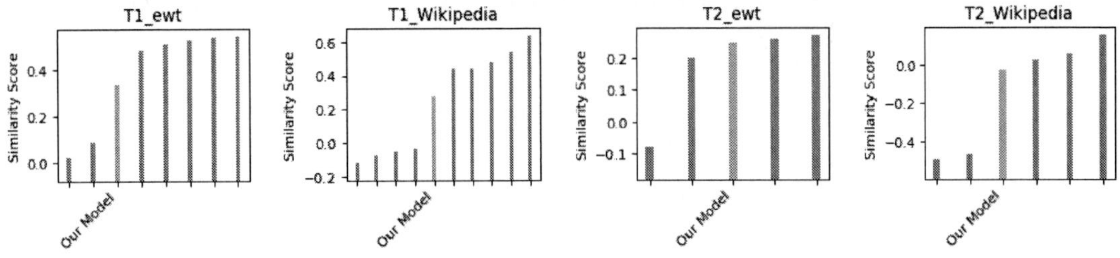

(b) Meaning Similarity

Figure 3: Human evaluation comparison of systems submitted in SR'20 on the `en_ewt-ud` and `en_Wikipedia` test sets for shallow (T1) and deep (T2) tracks evaluated based on their (a) readability and (b) meaning similarity.

A	Target	Shazad Khuram Ali , 27 , High Wycombe
	T1 output	Shazad Khuram , 27 High Wycombe ,
	T2 output	Shazad Khuram 27 High Wycombe Ali
B	Target	I hope you do n't mind , but I 've taken liberty to turn them into a web photo album at http://24.27.98.30/pictures/08-05_Garrett_Gayle_Bday .
	T1 output	I hope you do n't mind , but I 've taken liberty to turn them into a web photo album at http://24.98.30/pictures/08-05_garrett_gayle_bday .
	T2 output	I hope you do n't mind but I have taken liberty to turn them into a web photo album (http://24.98.30/pictures/08-05_garrett_gayle_bday.html) .

Table 2: Examples of unsuccessful outputs generated by our model on the shallow (T1) and deep (T2) tracks.

are some missing parts such as *27* or even extra parts such as *.html*. It should be noted that in Example B, the entire URL is considered as a single token.

5 Conclusion

In this work, we used a language model (text-to-text) to tackle the graph-to-text surface realization problem. We showed that using a pretrained encoder-decoder language model such as BART, can allow the model to reconstruct the tokens' orders and inflections in an end-to-end fashion without any modification in the network architecture. This shows that the pretrained language model is able to encode the graph information and map this representation into a human readable text. The results of the deep track showed that our proposed model achieved better performance compared with the systems submitted to SR'20 (Mille et al., 2020) where the model has to guess the functional words and morphological information. This high performance directly comes from the pretrained language model characteristics of BART. As for future work, we are planning to experiment with different graph linearization schemes. Also, we would like to use a multilingual language model such as mBART (Liu et al., 2020) on other languages as well as other language models. Finally, we would like to evaluate the incorporation of a copy mechanism (Gu et al., 2016) in generating long and complex tokens such as URLs.

Acknowledgements

The authors would like to thank the anonymous reviewers for their feedback on a previous version of this paper. This work was financially supported by the Natural Sciences and Engineering Research Council of Canada (NSERC).

References

Marie-Catherine de Marneffe, Timothy Dozat, Natalia Silveira, Katri Haverinen, Filip Ginter, Joakim Nivre, and Christopher D. Manning. 2014. Universal Stanford dependencies: A cross-linguistic typology. In *Proceedings of the Ninth International Conference on Language Resources and Evaluation (LREC-2014)*, pages 4585–4592, Reykjavik, Iceland, May. European Languages Resources Association (ELRA).

Wenchao Du and Alan W Black. 2019. Learning to order graph elements with application to multilingual surface realization. In *Proceedings of the 2nd Workshop on Multilingual Surface Realisation (MSR 2019)*, pages 18–24.

Nan Duan, Duyu Tang, Peng Chen, and Ming Zhou. 2017. Question generation for question answering. In *Proceedings of the 2017 Conference on Empirical Methods in Natural Language Processing*, pages 866–874.

Angela Fan, Claire Gardent, Chloé Braud, and Antoine Bordes. 2019. Using local knowledge graph construction to scale Seq2Seq models to multi-document inputs. In *Proceedings of the 2019 Conference on Empirical Methods in Natural Language Processing and the 9th International Joint Conference on Natural Language Processing (EMNLP-IJCNLP 2019)*, pages 4186–4196, Hong Kong, China, November. Association for Computational Linguistics.

Farhood Farahnak, Laya Rafiee, Leila Kosseim, and Thomas Fevens. 2019. The Concordia NLG Surface Realizer at SRST 2019. In *Proceedings of the 2nd Workshop on Multilingual Surface Realisation (MSR 2019)*, pages 63–67.

Y. Graham, Timothy Baldwin, A. Moffat, and J. Zobel. 2017. Can machine translation systems be evaluated by the crowd alone. *Nat. Lang. Eng.*, 23:3–30.

Jiatao Gu, Zhengdong Lu, Hang Li, and Victor O.K. Li. 2016. Incorporating copying mechanism in sequence-to-sequence learning. In *Proceedings of the 54th Annual Meeting of the Association for Computational Linguistics (Volume 1: Long Papers)*, pages 1631–1640, Berlin, Germany, August. Association for Computational Linguistics.

Hamza Harkous, Isabel Groves, and Amir Saffari. 2020. Have your text and use it too! End-to-end neural data-to-text generation with semantic fidelity. *arXiv preprint arXiv:2004.06577*.

Sepp Hochreiter and Jürgen Schmidhuber. 1997. Long short-term memory. *Neural computation*, 9(8):1735–1780.

Eduard Hovy, Gertjan van Noord, Guenter Neumann, and John Bateman. 1997. Language generation. *Survey of the State of the Art in Human Language Technology*, pages 131–146.

Mihir Kale. 2020. Text-to-text pre-training for data-to-text tasks. *arXiv preprint arXiv:2005.10433*.

Mike Lewis, Yinhan Liu, Naman Goyal, Marjan Ghazvininejad, Abdelrahman Mohamed, Omer Levy, Veselin Stoyanov, and Luke Zettlemoyer. 2020. BART: Denoising sequence-to-sequence pre-training for natural language generation, translation, and comprehension. In *Proceedings of the 58th Annual Meeting of the Association for Computational Linguistics*, pages 7871–7880, Online, July. Association for Computational Linguistics.

Yinhan Liu, Jiatao Gu, Naman Goyal, Xian Li, Sergey Edunov, Marjan Ghazvininejad, Mike Lewis, and Luke Zettlemoyer. 2020. Multilingual denoising pre-training for neural machine translation. *arXiv preprint arXiv:2001.08210*.

Ilya Loshchilov and Frank Hutter. 2019. Decoupled weight decay regularization. In *International Conference on Learning Representations*, Ernest N. Morial Convention Center, New Orleans, May.

Manuel Mager, Ramón Fernandez Astudillo, Tahira Naseem, Md Arafat Sultan, Young-Suk Lee, Radu Florian, and Salim Roukos. 2020. GPT-too: A language-model-first approach for AMR-to-text generation. In *Proceedings of the 58th Annual Meeting of the Association for Computational Linguistics (ACL-2020)*, pages 1846–1852, Online, July. Association for Computational Linguistics.

Alessandro Mazzei and Valerio Basile. 2019. The dipinfounito realizer at srst'19: Learning to rank and deep morphology prediction for multilingual surface realization. In *Proceedings of the 2nd Workshop on Multilingual Surface Realisation (MSR 2019)*, pages 81–87.

Simon Mille, Anja Belz, Bernd Bohnet, and Leo Wanner. 2018. Underspecified universal dependency structures as inputs for multilingual surface realisation. In *Proceedings of the 11th International Conference on Natural Language Generation*, pages 199–209, Tilburg University, The Netherlands, November. Association for Computational Linguistics.

Simon Mille, Anja Belz, Bernd Bohnet, Yvette Graham, and Leo Wanner. 2019. The Second Multilingual Surface Realisation Shared Task (SR'19): Overview and Evaluation Results. In *Proceedings of the 2nd Workshop on Multilingual Surface Realisation (MSR 2019), 2019 Conference on Empirical Methods in Natural Language Processing (EMNLP 2019)*, Hong Kong, China.

Simon Mille, Anya Belz, Bernd Bohnet, Thiago Castro Ferreira, Yvette Graham, and Leo Wanner. 2020. The third multilingual surface realisation shared task (SR'20): Overview and evaluation results. In *Proceedings of the 3nd Workshop on Multilingual Surface Realisation (MSR 2020)*, Dublin, Ireland, December. Association for Computational Linguistics.

Alec Radford, Jeffrey Wu, Rewon Child, David Luan, Dario Amodei, and Ilya Sutskever. 2019. Language models are unsupervised multitask learners. *OpenAI Blog*, 1(8).

Colin Raffel, Noam Shazeer, Adam Roberts, Katherine Lee, Sharan Narang, Michael Matena, Yanqi Zhou, Wei Li, and Peter J Liu. 2019. Exploring the limits of transfer learning with a unified text-to-text transformer. *arXiv preprint arXiv:1910.10683*.

Ehud Reiter and Robert Dale. 2000. *Building Natural Language Generation Systems*. Cambridge University Press, New York, NY, USA.

Ashish Vaswani, Noam Shazeer, Niki Parmar, Jakob Uszkoreit, Llion Jones, Aidan N Gomez, Łukasz Kaiser, and Illia Polosukhin. 2017. Attention is all you need. In *Advances in neural information processing systems (NIPS 2017)*, pages 5998–6008, Long Beach Convention Center, Long Beach.

Petar Veličković, Guillem Cucurull, Arantxa Casanova, Adriana Romero, Pietro Liò, and Yoshua Bengio. 2018. Graph Attention Networks. *International Conference on Learning Representations (ICLR 2018)*.

Oriol Vinyals, Meire Fortunato, and Navdeep Jaitly. 2015. Pointer Networks. In C. Cortes, N. D. Lawrence, D. D. Lee, M. Sugiyama, and R. Garnett, editors, *Advances in Neural Information Processing Systems 28 (NIPS 2015)*, pages 2692–2700. Curran Associates, Inc.

Thomas Wolf, Lysandre Debut, Victor Sanh, Julien Chaumond, Clement Delangue, Anthony Moi, Pierric Cistac, Tim Rault, Rémi Louf, Morgan Funtowicz, Joe Davison, Sam Shleifer, Patrick von Platen, Clara Ma, Yacine Jernite, Julien Plu, Canwen Xu, Teven Le Scao, Sylvain Gugger, Mariama Drame, Quentin Lhoest, and Alexander M. Rush. 2019. Huggingface's transformers: State-of-the-art natural language processing. *ArXiv*, abs/1910.03771.

Xiang Yu, Agnieszka Falenska, Marina Haid, Ngoc Thang Vu, and Jonas Kuhn. 2019. Imsurreal: Ims at the surface realization shared task 2019. In *Proceedings of the 2nd Workshop on Multilingual Surface Realisation (MSR 2019) (EMNLP 2019)*, pages 50–58, Hong Kong, China.

Yao Zhou, Cong Liu, and Yan Pan. 2016. Modelling sentence pairs with tree-structured attentive encoder. In *Proceedings of COLING 2016, the 26th International Conference on Computational Linguistics: Technical Papers*, pages 2912–2922, Osaka, Japan, December. The COLING 2016 Organizing Committee.

Association for Computational Linguistics
209 N. Eighth Street
Stroudsburg, Pennsylvania 18360

ISBN 978-1-7138-2832-7

CURRAN ASSOCIATES INC.
proceedings.com